FEARLESS IN OPPOSITION

P. Chidambaram is a former Union Minister of Finance and Home in the Government of India. Currently, he is a member of the Rajya Sabha and heads the Parliamentary Standing Committee on Home Affairs. He is an eminent lawyer practising in the Supreme Court. A public intellectual and author, he is the author of *Standing Guard: A Year in Opposition*—a collection of his essays published in 2016. He writes a weekly column on economy, politics, social issues, foreign policy and contemporary affairs in *The Indian EXPRESS*. A member of the Indian National Congress, the country's oldest political party, Chidambaram is a trustee of the Rajiv Gandhi Foundation.

Praise for the Book

'Mr Chidambaram's wisdom, knowledge and experience are eminently in display in this publication which brings together his commentary on some important issues of public policy pursued by the NDA government in 2016.'

—**Dr Manmohan Singh**,
Former Prime Minister of India

'In impeccable prose, Mr Chidambaram presents a scholarly survey of the events which jolted the economy and polity in 2016, tracing their origins and offering answers to them.'

—**Dr C. Rangarajan**,
Former Governor,
Reserve Bank of India

'As an eminent voice of the Opposition, Mr Chidambaram discharges his duty admirably well. *Fearless in Opposition* provides the reader with a counterpoint and critique of the mainstream narrative of the government in power on a wide range of issues.

—**Dr Rajiv Lall**,
Founder MD & CEO,
IDFC Bank

FEARLESS IN OPPOSITION

~Power and Accountability~

P. CHIDAMBARAM

RUPA

THE EXPRESS GROUP

EXPRESS BOOK™ SERIES

Published by
Rupa Publications India Pvt. Ltd 2017
7/16, Ansari Road, Daryaganj
New Delhi 110002

Sales Centres:

Allahabad Bengaluru Chennai
Hyderabad Jaipur Kathmandu
Kolkata Mumbai

Reprinted from *The Indian* EXPRESS

First published in hardback in 2017

ISBN: 978-81-291-4559-8

First impression 2017

10 9 8 7 6 5 4 3 2 1

Printed by Replika Press Pvt. Ltd, India

CONTENTS

FOREWORD

Raghuram G. Rajan
former Governor, Reserve Bank of India
Katherine Dusak Miller Distinguished Service Professor of Finance, Booth School of Business, University of Chicago

It is a privilege to write a foreword to this compendium of articles written by Mr Chidambaram in 2016. These articles are mainly written from the vantage point of a member of the 'loyal Opposition', that is a member of the non-governing party who examines the actions of the government critically, but is absolutely loyal to the source of government power. Even though as Reserve Bank of India (RBI) governor through much of last year I was part of the governing establishment, and therefore bear responsibility for some of Mr Chidambaram's concerns, I have no hesitation in saying that we need people of Mr Chidambaram's calibre to point out not just what he believes is going wrong, but what can be done to set it right.

With a few notable exceptions, the analysis of official policies one reads in the Indian press veers from being overly gentle to unduly harsh, with little in between. Constructive criticism is rare. In the articles penned by Mr Chidambaram, there is a lot of criticism (the reader can judge whether he opposes for the sake of opposing or whether there is merit in his arguments), but he also offers alternative pathways for the administration to follow. Not only do his suggestions draw from his formidable intellect and his vast experience in government, but they also reflect a deep understanding, even empathy, for the position the target of his criticism is in. After all, he has been in their position, where one has to act every day in an environment of global and domestic uncertainty, where there is no textbook showing the direction, and the information you need is dispersed, both within your ministry and amongst the wise men in the country.

Having seen Mr Chidambaram at work when I was the Chief Economic Adviser (CEA) at the Finance Ministry, I can attest to the care with which he made decisions. He rarely respected rank when discussing matters with his bureaucrats. What he was looking for was someone who knew the answer to the problem he had. Very quickly, with a few penetrating questions that got to the heart of the matter, he sorted out the pompous loudmouths from the truly knowledgeable. In meetings, if the secretary did not know, but a lowly deputy secretary knew the answer, the remaining conversation would be with the deputy secretary, while the secretary looked on. Perhaps bureaucrats were not happy that hierarchy had been breached, but decision making was more informed. After leaving office, I understand Mr Chidambaram follows the same procedure while writing the (few) articles where he does not have full domain expertise. He calls people who may know, informs himself, and then writes a clear and cogent piece. The nation benefited from his careful decision making when he was in office and benefits today from these pieces when he is in the Opposition.

What comes out in these pieces, for example, in the section on 'Nation and Nationalism', is not just a detailed analysis of current events, but also his fears about the populist nationalism that sometimes tends to overwhelm the fundamentally liberal idea of India he espouses. His articles on the difficult situation in Kashmir reflect the anguish of a liberal patriot at the ongoing tragedy there, and his policy suggestions are worth reflecting on. His commentary on the judiciary in India and what needs to be done to ensure that justice does not continue to be delayed and, thus denied, comes from his experience both as a lawyer as well as a Finance Minister. His articles on economic policy are thought-provoking—as always in India, there are enormous chasms between the intent of a policy announcement, its actual implementation and the effect on the intended beneficiary. All too often, as he points out, policy is not fully thought out because it does not take into account how real people behave, is rolled out all too slowly and ends up achieving too little of the intended aims. Once again, Mr Chidambaram's concerns come from someone who has the experience to recognise how things go wrong.

I particularly enjoyed reading his articles on the economic liberalisation in the early 1990s. I hope he will write more about the important roles played both by the then Prime Minister, P.V. Narasimha Rao, and the Finance Minister, Dr Manmohan Singh, as well as the surrounding cast such as Mr S. Venkitaramanan and Dr C. Rangarajan at the RBI. Mr Chidambaram, holding the commerce portfolio then, has been a central figure in Indian reforms, and one hopes for a lengthier autobiographical piece in the not too distant future. For now, I hope more such articles will whet our appetite for a 'fly on the wall' account of those momentous days in India's economic history.

To would-be reformers in India, Mr Chidambaram offers very useful advice in his article on economic freedom in India—instead of starting with the rules and regulations as they are, which usually means a nightmare of patches and fixes with the rationales buried in files in the deepest recesses of government, why not start with maximum freedom, and then put in only the regulations that are absolutely necessary? I can think of many candidates for this zero-based regulation. For example, an excellent one is the entire foreign exchange management regulation, which, I used to joke with my officers at the RBI, is there only to give them post-retirement employment as they help poor souls navigate its complexities. During my time at the RBI, we managed to streamline the rule book, but as India becomes more confident of its external position, more root-and-branch reform may be wise.

I should not spoil the articles for the reader by revealing too much. I hope Mr Chidambaram's articles will inform, challenge and entertain you as much as they did me. And I hope he will continue writing them—we are all wiser as a result.

3 January 2017

INTRODUCTION

This is the third collection of weekly columns that I have written in *The Indian Express*. The first two were separated by 10 years—2006 and 2016. The columns of 2015 were published in early 2016 under the title *Standing Guard: A Year in Opposition*. The book was received warmly by readers and reviewers. Another year in the Opposition in 2016, and part of the year as a member of the Rajya Sabha, gave me greater opportunity and freedom to comment on current affairs, and the output is this collection of 54 columns—one on every Sunday of the 52 weeks of the year, a special column immediately after the terrorist attack on the Air Force Station at Pathankot and one after the presentation of the Budget. After the success of the last collection, the publication of these columns was a natural outcome, and I hope that readers and reviewers will receive this book with equal warmth.

There is nothing more educative and rewarding for an active political person than to keenly observe the events as they unfold around him and sit down to write a reasoned comment on that. Writing a column is fraught with risks. Instant judgements could turn out to be terribly wrong. The actors in an event may have the power to change the narrative or reinterpret the event. Yet, the writer must write every week. He will pause, reflect on an event, gather the facts, commit his thoughts to paper and be prepared for any eventuality. I did precisely that through 2016. Never once did I forget that I was a member of the Opposition and my primary task was to perform the role of the Opposition in a democracy. That is why this collection is called *Fearless in Opposition: Power and*

Accountability. I ask readers to bear in my mind that I belong to the Opposition, not to some enemy camp, and I am performing my assigned role in a democracy.

Every day I observe, read and listen to a number of people. When I travel, which is quite frequent, I meet more people, listen to them and ask them questions. The subjects for the columns occur naturally. I choose the subject that is relevant and topical that week. Writing the first draft is the easy part; the difficult and time-consuming part is getting the data that will provide heft to the column. I have a fine researcher who helps me get the data and also takes the responsibility of verifying the data. The final task is to chisel the column to fit into the limit of 900 words. I spend a lot of time chopping and changing before I am satisfied that the column is readable and makes the point that I wished to make.

I like to write short sentences. Since the columns are written in English—which is neither my mother tongue nor the mother tongue of most of my readers—I think it makes sense to write in simple language and keep the sentences short. I place the facts and give my opinion in the comments and conclusions. I do not use harsh language, but in giving my opinion I do not mince words. I am not concerned about supporters and detractors. I just want more people to read the column and reflect on my comments and conclusions. I want to provoke debate without bitterness. I want to influence the decision makers without being disrespectful to them. I want to shape policy from the Opposition ranks.

I believe I have succeeded in a fair measure. My argument that the contrary view of the CEA should be overruled and the government should stick to the fiscal consolidation path prevailed. My insistence on a standard rate of Goods and Services Tax (GST) not exceeding 18 per cent appears to have been accepted. My formulation on the composition of the Monetary Policy Committee (MPC) with a casting vote (not a veto) to the Governor, RBI, was adopted by the government. These examples could be coincidences, nevertheless I am happy!

In 2016, the quality of public debate deteriorated. Apart from the usual pernicious campaigns (*ghar wapsi*, love jihad, etc.), new divisive demands were raised: say *Bharat Mata ki Jai*, don't question the 'surgical strike' by the Army, don't question demonetisation and so on. Few pause to reflect on the damage done by these self-appointed commissars to the democratic system which is founded on the principle of dialogue, debate and dissent. That reviled Bushism—'are you with me or are you against me'—seems to have found a home in India. When I encounter more divisive forces, I am provoked to speak more and write more. You should too.

Economics and the socio-economic advancement of all Indians remain my foremost concerns. The overarching goal of every government must be to wipe out poverty in India which, in the case of at least 100 million people, is abject poverty. In my view, at the end of its five-year tenure, a government will pass or fail on this test. Poverty is the worst affliction suffered by humankind, and the ultimate question is, 'How many people were lifted out of poverty?' It has been estimated that between 2004 and 2014, 140 million people were helped to get out of poverty. Our goal must be to lift at least one-half of that number, if not more, out of poverty in this five-year period (from 2014 to 2019) and improve on that achievement every five years.

I shall continue to speak and write as long as I can observe and reflect.

The columns in this collection have been grouped under sections. Within each section they are arranged in chronological order. Open any section, but please read all the columns in that section at one go. I believe you will get more than a flavour of the subject, how it unfolded during 2016, and how it affected you and your fellow citizens. It will help you recall events and gain a new perspective. The sections on 'Jammu and Kashmir' and 'Demonetisation' record the vicissitudes of the subject during the year and how I reacted to those developments. The section on the 'State of the Economy' captures the steady deterioration of the economy even as we were blinded by the dazzle of the GDP's growth rate. If, after reading a section, the reader is motivated to re-examine his/her long-held assumptions or beliefs, the purpose of my writing would have been achieved.

Thank you, and I hope you will enjoy the book.

NATION AND NATIONALISM

It is difficult to believe that the India in which we live today is the India of our dreams at the time of Independence. Every value that we cherished during the freedom struggle has been distorted beyond recognition. A simple slogan, '*Bharat Mata ki Jai*', that was raised to celebrate the eventual victory of the people of India (over British rule) has been twisted into a definition of who is a nationalist and who is not. Looking back, among the events that affected me most during 2016 were the tragic death of Rohith Vemula and the fires that were ignited in universities across the country. I refuse to accept any majoritarian attempt to define nationalism and patriotism. I refuse to accept that dissent is sedition.

'MY BIRTH IS MY FATAL ACCIDENT'

1 February 2016

'Reservation' for the socially and educationally backward classes in schools and colleges brought Rohith Chakravarthi Vemula to the University of Hyderabad, where he won a place in the general category as a PhD scholar in Life Sciences. 'Preservation' of the old social and economic order brought him death.

It is a miracle of our times that a Dalit, son of a security guard and a self-employed seamstress and instructor, could climb the ladder of education and be admitted as a scholar in a central university. On the way, he did not drop out. He was not pulled out by his parents to find low-paying work in order to bring a few rupees to support the family. He was not failed in school or college. He was not rusticated for some vague misdemeanour. He was not accused of a crime and thrown into prison. But he failed at the last hurdle.

Rohith and his friends held a protest against capital punishment and against the attack in Delhi on the screening of a documentary called *Muzaffarnagar Baaqi Hai*. The Akhil Bharatiya Vidyarthi Parishad (ABVP), which is the student wing of the Rashtriya Swayamsevak Sangh (RSS)/Bharatiya Janata Party (BJP), opposed the protest. Both groups were entitled to exercise their right to free speech as long as they were at a safe distance from each other. That is the essence of freedom and democracy in an open society.

What happened was the opposite. An ABVP leader, in his Facebook post, called the members of the Ambedkar Students Association (or ASA, which is a Dalit body) 'goons'. He was forced to apologise. He alleged that he had been beaten up by some members of the ASA, and the ABVP demanded action against them. It was a minor dispute between two groups that should have been resolved in the manner such minor disputes are resolved, but it was not.

Multiple Authors of a Script

Enter the Proctorial Board of the University. Enter the Minister who is also the local Member of Parliament (MP). Enter the Ministry of Human Resource Development. Enter the new Vice-Chancellor. Enter the Executive Council of the University. Enter the police.

The ABVP complained to the Minister/local MP, the Minister wrote to the Ministry of Human Resource Development, and the Ministry wrote to the University and followed it up with five reminders! In quick succession, the University instituted an enquiry, suspended five students (all Dalits) including Rohith, the Vice-Chancellor revoked the suspension temporarily and ordered another enquiry by a new committee, the next Vice-Chancellor scrapped the enquiry committee and ordered a fresh enquiry by a sub-committee of the Executive Council, the EC confirmed the suspension, and the students were directed to move out of the hostel. The script of a tragedy was being written by multiple authors, but none paused to reflect on the consequences of the action they had been pressured to take. The tragedy indeed occurred on 17 January 2016, when Rohith hanged himself.

Entitled vs Disentitled

Who has the power to move a Minister/local MP to write a letter to the Minister of Human Resource Development alleging (based purely on hearsay) that the ASA was indulging in 'casteist and anti-national activities'? Who has the power to move the Ministry to forward the letter to the University and write five reminders within a few weeks? Only the

SLOGANS, PATRIOTS AND ANTI-NATIONALS

27 March 2016

Slogans and elections are inseparable companions. When the Lok Sabha election of 2014 was imminent, the BJP named Mr Narendra Modi as its candidate for Prime Minister, and the candidate almost immediately began to popularise the slogans that would eventually define the election: Achhe din aanewale hain,[1] Kaala dhan wapasi,[2] Sabka saath, sabka vikas,[3] and many others. Along with other things going the party's way, the slogans catapulted the BJP to power.

Today, those slogans sound hollow. No one dares raise them for fear of becoming an object of derision. But with more state elections round the corner, how can we do without new slogans?

The new slogan is a resurrection of an old slogan: '*Bharat Mata ki Jai*'. It means 'Victory to Mother India'. But it is a slogan that, if raised every day, will leave most people wondering why it should be raised. It was appropriate when Indian troops recaptured Tiger Hill, but on other occasions it would be hardly relevant. Consider, for example, raising it at the end of an investors' meeting or a lecture on judicial reforms or the launch of a book! The audience will be bemused.

---

[1]Good days are coming

[2]Bring back black money

[3]With everyone, development for everyone

'Project Nationalism'

Lest you make a mistake, I may caution you that the new champions of the slogan have a purpose in mind: they use the slogan to peddle the specious argument that those who raise the slogan—and only those—are patriots, and those who do not are not patriots and are, therefore, anti-national.

That is a sure way to divide the people. Hoping to reap electoral gains, the BJP has consciously adopted the plank of nationalism.

We, the people of India, have formed a Union of States and given to ourselves a Constitution. It is perfectly legitimate to ask everyone to be loyal to the Union and to the Constitution. That is the duty of every citizen, but no government has the right to ask its citizens to do anything more.

'Project Nationalism' seeks to bludgeon the people to submerge their individual identities in a presumed national identity—that there is one history, one ethnicity, one race, one culture and one system of values that binds the people of India. It is this presumed national identity that emboldens self-appointed leaders to lay down rules on what one should eat or wear or read or view; or who one should love or marry; or who should be included or excluded or punished.

If we accept the BJP's definition of nationalism, it will take only a few short steps to the conclusion that one religion is superior to others; that one language should be taught to all children; that one culture should permeate national life; or that one set of values should inform the lives of all the people.

State and Nation

The BJP's attempt to define a nationalist as one who will say '*Bharat Mata ki Jai*' is a gross distortion of history. In his *Discovery of India*, Jawaharlal Nehru wrote that *Bharat Mata* was essentially the people of India and victory to her meant victory to the people of India. He led us to adopt an inclusive and democratic Constitution. The Constitution was a bold experiment in reshaping a historically inegalitarian society into an inclusive and democratic State where everyone could have a place of honour and dignity without sacrificing one's individual identity.

State and nation are not synonyms. The 'State' is a compact among the people that is sealed by a Constitution and the laws that are willingly enacted by the people. A 'nation' is a historical concept shaped by the history, the struggles and the experience of a people. The United Kingdom is a State, but the Scots, the Irish and the Welsh will not refer to themselves as English. Belgium is another State where two nationalities coexist. The communists have for a long time held a distinct view on nationalities.

Nationalism as a simple expression of love or respect for the nation poses no problem. If, befitting the occasion, such love or respect may be expressed by raising a slogan, there are many slogans that have adorned our history: *Vande Mataram*, *Bharat Mata ki Jai, Inquilab Zindabad* and *Jai Hind.*

To choose one over the others and make the raising of that slogan as the test of loyalty or patriotism is a pernicious attempt to manipulate or control the people. It deserves to be rejected.

A Step Short of Fascism

Ultra-nationalism is divisive and not very different from fascism. Read this passage from *The Doctrine of Fascism* (attributed to Mussolini):

'Liberalism denied the State in the name of the individual; Fascism reasserts the right of the State as expressing the real essence of the individual... Fascism stands for liberty, and for the only liberty worth having, the liberty of the State and of the individual within the State.'

That is the antithesis of our idea of liberty enshrined in the Constitution. In a celebrated judgement upholding the rights of children (who belonged to a religious denomination, Jehovah's Witnesses) to stand up respectfully but not sing when the National Anthem was played, the Supreme Court noted: 'Our tradition teaches tolerance; our philosophy preaches tolerance; our Constitution practises tolerance; let us not dilute it.' The question that each one of us must ask oneself is, 'Do I value my liberty?' I have the liberty to raise the slogan '*Bharat Mata ki Jai*' depending upon the occasion, and I shall do so with pride. I also have the liberty not to do so. And I shall not allow anyone, and certainly not the State, to define if I am a nationalist or not.

IF WE KILL DISSENT, WE WILL KILL LIBERTY

18 October 2016

According to the Director General of Military Operations (DGMO), there were surgical strikes on 'launch pads' situated 'along' the Line of Control (LoC) in Pakistan Occupied Kashmir (PoK). I believe the DGMO, as we have always believed past Directors General and past Chiefs of the Army. The DGMO said that 'significant casualties' had been inflicted on the enemy, but he did not give any number. He was at pains to emphasise that there were 'no plans for further continuation'. The nation applauded him and the Army.

But somewhere in the translation, the message was lost. It was certainly lost on one person who ought to have maintained restraint—the Defence Minister. His utterances since the strike have been over the top, gross exaggerations, and invited ridicule even from quarters that generally supported the government.

Truth Is the Casualty

Pause here and reflect. Is there any truth in, or justification for, the Defence Minister's statement that:

- like Hanuman, the Army did not know their prowess until I pointed out to them their strength and capacity;

- such an action has never been done before and this is the first surgical strike by the Army;
- nowhere in the world has such an operation been done with such a degree of success;
- thirty years of helplessness and frustration have been lifted by this action and the people erupted in joy.

Much of the above could be brushed aside as the enthusiasm of a first-time central minister, if they had no consequences. Unfortunately, there will be consequences. That is why, I think, the Prime Minister had to caution his ministers not to indulge in 'chest thumping'. Who did the Prime Minister have in mind, if not the Defence Minister? But Mr Parrikar is not deterred. He is on a roller-coaster ride and totally unmindful of the fact that he has made a spectacle of himself.

Dividends of Strategic Restraint

As the Army's spokesman said, 'This is not the first time and this will not be the last time'. The LoC is a line of truce. It is in the mutual interest of India and Pakistan that the understanding to maintain ceasefire, reached in 2003, is maintained by both sides as fully as possible and as long as possible. If the understanding is breached by one side, it will invite retaliation by the other. Both Armies know this simple rule. In the past too, there have been breaches and retaliations. No less a person than General Bikram Singh, a former Army Chief, confirmed this recently. No less a person than Mr Shivshankar Menon, a former National Security Adviser (NSA), explained the nature of such cross-LoC actions. And *The Hindu* dug into the records and published an undeniable report on Operation Ginger (2011).

The UPA government followed a policy of 'strategic restraint'. No one had seriously questioned the policy at that time. It yielded dividends in the matter of reducing the level of violence in Jammu and Kashmir (J&K) (see table).

Year	*Incidents*	*Forces Killed*	*Civilians Killed*	*Terrorists Killed*
2004	2,565	281	707	976
2005	1,990	189	557	917
2006	1,667	151	389	591
2007	1,092	110	158	472
2008	708	75	91	339
2009	499	78	71	239
2010	488	69	47	232
2011	340	33	31	100
2012	220	38	11	50
2013	170	53	15	67
2014	222	47	28	110
2015	208	39	22	108

Only a person who is unusually obtuse will say that the policy of the UPA government was muddle-headed or wrong. The situation began to change in 2014, yet the number of incidents and number of fatalities were under control.

Gurdaspur, Pathankot, Pampore and Uri brought about a qualitative change. The government of the day is entitled to review the policy of strategic restraint. It is also entitled to authorise cross-LoC action and, in its wisdom, take political ownership of the Army's action. What the government is not entitled to do is indulge in exaggeration and vilification of previous governments and their policies. That is the fault of the Defence Minister.

Criticism Is Liberty

There will be criticism of the Defence Minister. There will be criticism of the modified (and seemingly muscular) policy. There will be criticism that the government had not weighed the consequences of raising an Army-level 'tactical operation' to a government-level 'policy instrument'. Alternatives will be suggested.

Questions will be asked. When did 'along' the LoC become 'deep strikes'? Is not 'launch pad' associated with missiles? What is the difference between 'cross-LoC action' and 'surgical strike'? Did the DGMO give the number of casualties?

Criticism—and questions—will enrich public debate. It is the essence of liberty. The events that will unfold in the weeks and months to come may prove the critic to be right or to be wrong. Even if he is proven wrong, the critic is not unpatriotic or anti-national.

Freedom movements have been criticised. Wartime leaders have been defeated. Civil wars have been fought among citizens of a country with neither side forfeiting the right to be called patriotic. Through all the turbulence, the one value that has stood out among people who cherish liberty is freedom of speech and expression. If you kill that voice, you will kill liberty.

I am afraid that there are too many people out there—in political parties, in governments, in the media, in the social media—who seem determined to kill the voice of liberty.

NO QUESTIONS PLEASE, WE ARE PATRIOTS

7 November 2016

A new social and political code is in the making: Don't ask questions. It is the exact opposite of the ethos that was considered absolutely necessary in a democracy and which led to the enactment of the Right to Information Act (RTI Act)—that transparency and openness are the hallmarks of a democracy and that information, with few exceptions, must be available to the public. The RTI Act has made a world of difference to the process of decision making, reduced arbitrariness and exposed corruption, and is a great weapon in fighting injustice. In the past, governments had got away with plain lies because there was no way to call their bluff. (Courts did intervene occasionally, but they were constrained by the lack of judges, backlog of cases and paucity of time. The sheer volume of work has overwhelmed the judicial system.) The RTI Act has been a game changer.

Tradition of Questioning

The same principle informs the Question Hour in Parliament. Ask a question, and the minister is bound to answer, truthfully, within 14 days. Supplementary questions can be put to the minister on the floor of the House and she is bound to answer. Many ministers are caught out in Question Hour. A minister who has provided a wrong answer is liable to be hauled up for breach of privilege. A vigilant Prime Minister, if he sits through Question Hour for a whole session, can separate the wheat from the chaff among his ministers.

If questions had not been asked, the world would be flat, homosexuality would be a disease, and the woman alone should bear the blame if a couple were childless. Gravity would not have been discovered, relativity would be a crazy man's tale and flying would be only for the birds.

Socrates told his pupils to question everything and a good teacher will tell the same thing today to her class. Thomas Becket, canonised later by a Catholic Pope, questioned his king; Martin Luther questioned the Catholic Church's dogmas. *Vishista-advaita* was born because it questioned the philosophy of *advaita*.

Mahatma Gandhi questioned the professed authority of the white man to rule over the Indian people; 50 years later, Martin Luther King questioned the professed superiority of the white citizen over the black citizen.

Deng Xiao Ping questioned the Communist–Maoist orthodoxy and ushered in economic liberalisation in China; the Maoists question the inequality and inequity aggravated by economic liberalisation in India.

Every war—Vietnam to Iraq to Syria—has been revisited and questioned. The Henderson–Brooks report questioned the conduct of the India–China war of 1962.

The New Code

The great tradition of asking questions is under threat. The rules of the new code are:

1. Do not ask questions.
2. If you ask questions, you are anti-national.
3. Your question will be turned on its head to mean something totally perverse.
4. Your questions will be met with irrelevant questions.
5. The irrelevant questions will be answered, not your questions.

There are other gems that have not yet been elevated to the status of rules but they may soon be. Here are two: Asking questions is not good culture (Mr Kiren Rijiju). Asking questions is cheap politics (Mr Venkaiah Naidu).

In the last year, there has been a determined attempt to shut out questions and shut up people who asked questions. When Akhlaq was lynched by a mob, the question was who gave the mob the right to kill him. That question was replaced by 'Did Akhlaq's family keep beef in their house?' Socrates would have asked, 'What has the family keeping meat of any kind got to do with the criminal act of a mob playing the role of judge, jury, prosecutor and executioner?'

When Rohith Vemula explained in his last testament why he took his own life, all questions were brushed aside. The only question that was allowed was, 'Was Rohith Vemula a Dalit or a non-Dalit?' The judge answered dutifully that he was not a Dalit. Socrates would have asked, 'Did the answer throw light upon the fundamental issues of discrimination and oppression raised by the young scholar in his last letter?'

Taking Refuge in Lies

Questions were asked about the chest-thumping over the cross-border action by the Army. They were turned on their head as if the questions were about the Army's competence and truthfulness. The new rules took over and those who asked the questions were branded anti-national.

There are questions about the veracity of the official version (or versions) of the Bhopal jailbreak in which eight prisoners escaped after brutally killing a head constable, Ramashankar Yadav. Hours later, the police claimed that all eight had been killed in an 'encounter'. Was it true or fake? The people of India have, regrettably, tolerated encounters of both kinds. It is the law that does not tolerate fake encounters. Even in the case of a genuine encounter, the law obliges the government to register an FIR and hold a thorough and independent enquiry. The Government of Madhya Pradesh is stoutly resisting an enquiry and employing every trick and lie to forestall one. Sample these: 'Accused' in cases of terrorism have become 'terrorists'. Undertrials have become convicted prisoners. Prison food has become chicken biryani.

But let me tell you, the law will catch up and there will be an enquiry. I cannot say whether the truth will come out of the enquiry but, at least, the questions will be asked.

A GOVERNMENT DISCONNECTED

'Government *of* the people' is not a clever turn of phrase; it is an essential attribute of the parliamentary form of democracy. Every government is elected *by* the people, claims to govern *for* the people, but quite often ceases to be a government *of* the people. The ruling class is derisively called the Establishment. It is amazing how quickly a government can disconnect itself from the people who voted it into office. When this 'disconnect' happens, the worst sufferers are the poor, the oppressed and the disadvantaged sections of the people. Every change of government is an anxious attempt by the people to re-establish the 'connect' with the elected government.

IT IS NOT YET THE TURNING POINT

22 May 2016

Sometimes, the expected masquerades as the unexpected. Sober reflection had told us many months ago that the governments in Assam and Kerala would be voted out and new governments voted in, and that a change would also happen in Puducherry. That in West Bengal, the TMC would be returned to power overcoming the unusual (but understandable) tactical alliance between the Congress and the Left parties.

The only enigmatic state was Tamil Nadu. Will Ms Jayalalithaa (All India Anna Dravida Munnetra Kazhagam [AIADMK]) defy history and be returned for a second consecutive term? Or, will Mr Karunanidhi (Dravida Munnetra Kazhagam [DMK]) defy age and become the Chief Minister at 92 years?

As it turned out, the election results were as expected a few months ago—that is, before the spin masters and the pollsters took over and created a mystery around the elections.

The two national parties have much to introspect about. The hard truth is that neither of them has a truly national footprint today. The Congress has a limited presence in the Hindi heartland and the BJP has a nominal presence in the southern and eastern states. A large space is occupied by one-state parties.

Of the two, it is the Congress that has more reasons to worry. In the case of the BJP, it will be in office at the Centre for another three years and it can boast that it has claimed one major state (Assam) without losing any. On the contrary, the Congress is now in office in only one major state (Karnataka), having lost two in this round of elections.

Both parties have seven months to rework their strategies before they face crucial elections in seven states—including the prize catch of Uttar Pradesh. Winning Uttar Pradesh, at present, is a toss-up between two powerful regional players, the Samajwadi Party (SP) and the Bahujan Samaj Party (BSP). Both national parties have three states each to defend: the BJP will defend Goa, Gujarat and Punjab, and the Congress will defend Himachal Pradesh, Manipur and Uttarakhand. The scales between the two national parties are pretty even at this point of time.

I am an ardent supporter of the case for 'national' parties because I think building a nation and fostering a sense of nationhood require the presence of at least two national parties that can form, or lead, a government at the Centre.

Crucial Mistakes

Both the BJP and the Congress made crucial mistakes in the run-up to the 2016 elections. The BJP made the mistake of 'creating' a political party out of the Sree Narayana Dharma Paripalana (SNDP) in Kerala and aligning with that party, hoping to divide the people of Kerala on religious lines. It won just one seat. The Congress made the mistake of not aligning with the All India United Democratic Front (AIUDF) and the Bodoland People's Front (BoPF) in Assam, fearing that such an alliance would polarise the voters which, in any event, happened thanks to the AIUDF's rhetoric, and ensured a comfortable victory for the BJP.

After the heat and dust of the elections settle, both the BJP and the Congress would have to reorganise themselves for the big battle of 2019. Both have huge responsibilities during the next three years. In the case of the BJP, it must demonstrate that it has the capacity to deliver 8-plus per cent growth, create jobs for the millions who are unemployed, and keep social peace and harmony. In the case of the Congress, it must demonstrate that it has the capacity to become, once again, the natural party of governance. It must also rebuild the party from the village/town unit to the block unit to the district unit to the state unit, many of which exist today only on paper.

I am hardly in a position to advise either party. To the BJP, I am a member of the party in Opposition and hence must be regarded as a suspect! To the Congress, I am a member of that party and hence must remain discreet!

Unsolicited Advice

Nevertheless, I have decided to advise both national parties. What I will say now is what I have said before (on the dates in parentheses).

To the BJP, I say the following:

- India's new 'normal' for GDP growth seems to be 7 per cent. In order to break away from the new 'normal', the government must summon the vision and courage to do bold structural reforms (*à la* 1991–92) as well as the grace and humility to engage the Opposition and accommodate their views (22 November 2015).
- Mr Modi can pause, take stock, pull back and steer the party on the path of good governance and development (15 November 2015).

To the Congress, I say the following:

- There will always be a número uno, but it is good to present a picture of a collective leadership. King Arthur had his round table.
- Secondly, the Congress must constitute or reconstitute the committees at the block level. It is a task that can, starting from scratch, be accomplished in 12 months or less.
- Thirdly, the Congress must communicate its views to its cadres and to the people every day in Hindi, English and other Indian languages (15 February 2015).
- And I would add, fourthly, the Congress must rewrite its policy platform on the key social and economic issues in a manner that would appeal to the age group of 15 to 35 years.

After Delhi and Bihar, it was believed that the five elections of 2016 will be the turning point. Nothing of that sort has happened, but the results of 2016 hint that the elections of 2017 may turn out to be the decisive turning point.

FAKE ENCOUNTER WITH FACTS, FAKE CONTROVERSY

19 June 2016

Ishrat Jahan and three others were killed by the Gujarat police in an encounter. Was it a genuine encounter or a fake encounter? I do not know the answer.

There are others who claim to know the answer. I am astonished by the certitude of some of my fellow citizens that the encounter was a genuine encounter. None of them had access to the case diary or the statements of witnesses or the forensic reports. None of them had read the charge sheet in the case. Yet, they are absolutely certain that the four persons who were killed were terrorists and the encounter was genuine!

Kasab vs Akhlaq

Little do they realise that their 'process of reasoning' will be the death knell of the rule of law.

I am proud to swear by the principle that 'every person shall be presumed to be innocent unless proven guilty in a fair trial in a court of law'. The day we jettison this principle will be the day that marks the beginning of the end of the rule of law in this country.

The government did not jettison the principle in the case of Ajmal

Kasab. A mob jettisoned the principle in the case of Mohammad Akhlaq. The Ishrat Jahan case is a good case to test our allegiance to the principle.

Central intelligence agencies had provided intelligence inputs to the Gujarat police that Ishrat Jahan and three others were terrorists or linked to terrorists. It was the duty of the Gujarat police to act on the inputs, apprehend the suspects, gather evidence, charge them and bring them before a court of law. However, what happened was the exact opposite.

On 15 June 2004, Ishrat Jahan and three others were killed. The police claimed that it was a genuine encounter. Ishrat Jahan's mother, Shamima Kausar, alleged that it was a fake encounter and that the four persons were killed while they were in police custody. A Special Judge ordered an enquiry by the Metropolitan Magistrate.

Judge, SIT and CBI

On 7 September 2009, Judge Tamang, after an enquiry, concluded that the killings took place in a fake encounter. His findings were chilling:

- that the four persons were killed while they were in police custody, on the night of 14 June 2004;
- that they were killed by shots fired from a close distance while they were sitting in a car; and
- that the weapons from which the shots were fired were unlicensed and illegal.

By order dated 12 August 2010, the High Court of Gujarat constituted a Special Investigation Team (SIT). After investigation, the SIT concluded that the encounter was a fake encounter.

On 1 December 2011, the High Court ordered that the case shall be taken over by the Central Bureau of Investigation (CBI). The CBI investigated the case and concluded that the encounter was a fake encounter. On 3 July 2013, the CBI filed a charge sheet against seven police officers. Consistent with the principle that I hold inviolable, I am prepared to say that the police officers shall be presumed to be innocent unless proven guilty at the trial.

From the Further Affidavit

2. I am making this further Affidavit in view of subsequent developments in relation to issues connected with the Petition, and to clarify apprehensions expressed in regard to the Affidavit filed by the Union of India as well to refute attempts to misinterpret portions of the Affidavit.

5. I respectfully submit that the Central Government in the said Affidavit did not address any issue relating to the merits or otherwise of the police action. It was essentially concerned with dealing with the allegations relating to the 'intelligence inputs' which are available with the Central Government and which are shared on a regular basis with the State Governments. The primary concern of the Central Government was to see that the inputs gathered by the Indian Security Agencies and their efforts were not discredited. I say that it should be clear to all that such inputs do not constitute conclusive proof and it is for the State Government and the State Police to act on such inputs. The Central Government is in no way concerned with such action nor does it condone or endorse any unjustified or excessive action.

The Affidavits

The central government's role in the case was limited to filing an affidavit in the High Court in the case instituted by Shamima Kausar. An affidavit—the first affidavit—was filed on 6 August 2009. A month later, the report of Judge Tamang was released. There was an uproar in Gujarat and elsewhere. The Gujarat police defended the encounter citing the 'intelligence inputs' by misinterpreting the affidavit. Therefore, it was necessary to clarify the affidavit. Accordingly, a 'further affidavit' was filed on 29 September 2009. The affidavit was vetted and approved by the Attorney General of India. Paragraphs 2 and 5 were the key paragraphs. The important clarification was intelligence 'inputs do not constitute conclusive proof and it is for the State government and the State police to act on such inputs'. No government can pronounce anyone guilty or innocent. No one can declare that Ishrat Jahan and three others were 'terrorists'. By the same principle, no one can pronounce that the seven persons charge sheeted by the CBI were guilty of murder. Those powers belong exclusively to the courts.

Now, please read the two paragraphs. Please tell me which sentence, phrase or word in the said paragraphs, or in the whole 'further affidavit', was wrong—ethically or legally.

The real controversy is not about the affidavits, it is about the encounter on the night of 14/15 June 2004. Was it a fake encounter? I do not know. But is the controversy over the affidavits a fake controversy? Undoubtedly, yes.

DISCONNECT BETWEEN GOVERNMENT AND PEOPLE

3 July 2016

The people of the United Kingdom (UK) have decided to leave the European Union (EU). More accurately, a divided people of a disunited kingdom have voted by a majority of less than 4 per cent to quit a Union they had joined 43 years ago. Scotland, Northern Ireland and London were on one side of the divide, while England and Wales were on the other. Most young people voted to 'remain' while most older people voted to 'leave'.

The vote to leave may not unravel the EU, but it threatens to unravel the UK and has raised the question: 'Why did Prime Minister Cameron decide to hold a referendum?'

The UK is a parliamentary democracy, not a plebiscitary democracy. Policies and laws are made by Parliament, not by the people directly. Mr Cameron gambled on a referendum to quell an internal rebellion within the Conservative party and failed. The cardinal rule of politics is that 'never call a referendum (or a vote) unless you are certain that the outcome will be in your favour'. Mr Cameron violated the rule. Why? Because he assumed, like many elected leaders, that since he enjoyed the support of a majority in Parliament, he enjoyed the support of a majority of the people as well. That was a fatal mistake.

The people's vote is defined by the time and the context of the vote.

But times change; the context also may change. The majority that a leader won in a parliamentary election will endure for the duration of the term, but the leader may have lost the support of the people at large.

The leader may indeed be standing where he stood, but the ground may have shifted under his feet. Most Prime Ministers are loath to accept the fact that they may have lost the support of the people—at least on some crucial issues.

Mr Cameron miscalculated his support on issues such as immigration, jobs and multiculturalism. He was absolutely right in taking the position—as any decent, thinking man would—that Britain was a better country because it was multicultural; that jobs that the British people did not want to do had to be done by someone and the immigrants were willing to do those jobs; and that being part of the EU, despite the obtrusive and oppressive bureaucracy in Brussels, was good for the British economy. Many people thought like Mr Cameron, but many more thought otherwise.

As a result of the vote taken on 23 June 2016, British politics has imploded. The UK is effectively without a Prime Minister and without a Leader of the Opposition.

31 per cent vs 69 per cent

Prime Minister Modi's party, the BJP, was voted into office by 31 per cent of the people who took part in the voting. A plurality of voters, not a simple majority, preferred his party. In a first-past-the-post system, that 31 per cent was sufficient to give the party a majority in the Lok Sabha. Unquestionably, it is a legitimate majority. Yet, I am sure, the Prime Minister has often pondered on how to wean some of the 69 per cent to his side.

What the 31 per cent and the 69 per cent will do is not predictable. One thing, however, is certain: the two numbers will not remain frozen for five years. There could be an erosion of support for the government, there could be an accretion. Going by the results of elections held in different states since 2014, my guess is that Mr Narendra Modi has perhaps retained the support of the 31 per cent, but has not won over any of the

69 per cent that had voted against the BJP in 2014.

Is There a Disconnect?

There is another way to look at the dichotomy between a majority in Parliament and a majority among the people. Suppose we put the following questions to the electorate and ask them to vote on each question (a sort of a referendum):

1. Do you approve of the permission given to the Pakistani investigation team to visit Pathankot without extracting a promise from Pakistan to allow an Indian investigation team to visit Pakistan?
2. Do you approve of the Prime Minister's silence in the wake of provocative utterances by some of his ministers and Members of Parliament?
3. Do you approve of the Prime Minister's comment that Mahatma Gandhi National Rural Employment Guarantee Act (MGNREGA) was 'a monument to the failure of the Congress party'?
4. Do you approve of the manner in which the government handled the issue of a second term for the Governor, RBI?
5. Do you approve of the appointments made by the government to key institutions/bodies such as the Indian Council of Historical Research (ICHR), Film and Television Institute of India (FTII), National Institute of Fashion Technology (NIFT), Central Board of Film Certification and Indira Gandhi National Centre for the Arts?
6. Do you approve of the government's decision to pass the GST law without putting a cap on the rate of tax, which is an indirect tax and, therefore, a regressive tax?

I concede that none of these questions is as seminal as the 'Remain or Leave' question that was before the British people, but it may be useful to the government to find out the measure of support. My guess is that on each of these issues the government had (or has) the support of less than 31 per cent. The wise course is to make corrections to avoid a disconnect with the people.

DALITS ARE RIGHT—ENOUGH IS ENOUGH

6 October 2016

On 11 July 2016, a video of cow vigilantes mercilessly beating up seven Dalit men for skinning a dead cow in Una district, Gujarat, came to light. In protest against the incident, many Dalits have refused to handle cow carcasses. The *gau rakshaks*[1] should be happy, but they are not. Non-Dalits, presumably including *gau rakshaks*, have retaliated with more violence against Dalits—this time for not picking up cow carcasses—in Samter (16 August), Bhavra (20 August) and Rajkot (24 August), all in Gujarat.

Herein lies the Dalit dilemma—he is damned if he does and he is damned if he doesn't.

The bane of Hindu society is *varna*, the four-tier arrangement said to be sanctified by the scriptures. The arrangement encompassed the majority and assigned them places, but it also excluded a large number. The excluded were the outcasts or the untouchables. Inequality by birth was the basis of the arrangement. That inequality stayed with you throughout your life. Violence against Dalits is the punishment for disobeying the rules of the arrangement. Rohith Vemula summed it up: 'My birth is my fatal accident.'

[1]Protectors of the cow

The Dalit Mobilisation

The Dalits have decided that enough is enough. They have decided to mobilise. The scale of social mobilisation of Dalits in Gujarat and Maharashtra, and to some extent in other parts of the country, has not been seen in recent times. Although much of the media is not covering them, massive rallies and marches are being held. There is palpable anger in the community because of the sense of impunity with which they are being subjected to violence in certain parts of the country. According to the National Commission for Scheduled Castes, in 2015, Gujarat reported the highest crime rate against Dalits, followed by Chhattisgarh and Rajasthan.

Dalits are angry about the hollowness of the current hyper-nationalism where everything about India is called great and every criticism is labelled as anti-national. They are angry about the way the Una incident and other such incidents are being dismissed as isolated or as conspiracies. It is noteworthy that the boycott of cow carcasses, the rallies and the marches have happened through social, and not political, mobilisation.

After a long period of silence, the Prime Minister spoke on 6 August 2016. He said, 'I get so angry at those who are into the *gau rakshak* business.... I have seen that some people are into crimes all night and wear the garb of *gau rakshaks* in the day.' The very next day, at a rally, he said, 'You can shoot me rather than target the Dalits.' This is a strange statement for a Prime Minister: he should use the enormous powers of his office to punish the perpetrators of violence.

Change Is Agonisingly Slow

Change is taking place, but it is agonisingly slow. In urban areas, where economic and professional identities usually take precedence, and in parts of India where social movements have brought about change, the majority of Hindus do not feel passionate about the caste order. Many Hindus may still prefer marriages within the caste, but have friends among Dalits. Many may express angst about the reservation system, but do not begrudge the limited preference to Dalits in educational institutions and in some jobs.

However, there is a section of Hindu society that continues to look back with nostalgia at the days of caste domination. Many of them have read a sign of approval in the BJP's victory in 2014. The cow vigilantes are the latest manifestation of centuries of a supremacist ideology. The flurry of bans on cow slaughter and beef consumption, and the aggressive majoritarian narrative, have given them fresh wind.

Few people saw the casteist agenda more clearly than Dr Ambedkar and 'Periyar' E.V. Ramasamy. Both were pessimistic about the reformation of Hindu society. Dr Ambedkar did not think that Dalits could find dignity within the fold of the Hindu religion and urged them to convert to Buddhism. Periyar's way was atheism and rationalism. The third way is the reform of the Hindu social order and accelerating the trends that will usher in a new social order—education, industrialisation, urbanisation, communication and technological advance.

The Constitutional Goal

For the Hindu hyper-nationalists, the idea of a 'Hindu' nation is superior to the idea of a constitutional democratic republic. They will sweep the pains of caste history under the carpet. They think that to uphold the idea of a 'Hindu' nation, it is necessary to underplay its flaws and hide the price that is paid by millions of Dalits and the minorities. On the other hand, the Constitution-makers did not deny the existence of these problems: they acknowledged the prevalence of caste differences and discrimination and formulated what they believed would be intermediate solutions, such as reservation for the Scheduled Castes and rights of minorities.

The real focus of the Constitution is to secure a set of natural rights that every Indian should enjoy, irrespective of the historical injustices. It is to make caste, religion and gender irrelevant to citizenship and citizens' rights.

The project of creating this sense of equal citizenship is still a work-in-progress in this vast and complex land. Hindu hyper-nationalism, which is a form of majoritarianism, is at odds with the constitutional project. The conflict is playing out, in an increasingly violent manner, before our eyes. The consequences of a long-drawn conflict will be terrible for the country and its progress towards the goal of a peaceful and prosperous nation.

JAMMU AND KASHMIR

India prides itself in being a teacher, a preacher and a peace maker, but India has failed miserably in making peace with the seven million-strong people of the Kashmir valley. Successive governments have pursued policies that can be described as myopic and inhuman. Sane voices were raised from time to time, but they fell silent amidst the cacophony of words like accession, State, territory, sovereignty and territorial integrity. Why are we unable to comprehend the desire of a people with unique characteristics—land, language, religion, culture, history and suffering—for a large measure of autonomy? Why is our vision different when we look to the South (Sri Lanka) and when we look to the North (Jammu & Kashmir)?

The two initiatives that helped change perceptions were:

- the visit of an all-party delegation to J&K and the marathon dialogue it held with numerous groups and persons, and
- the appointment of three interlocutors who engaged the civil society of J&K in a manner that had not been done before.

The measures taken before and after these two initiatives helped to bring down, considerably, the level of violence that had marked the recent history of that State, as can be seen from the following:

Incidents of Violence

Year	*Incidents*	*Civilians killed*	*Security personnel killed*
2001	4,522	919	536
2014	222	28	47

Right and Wrong Responses

A large section of the youth in the Kashmir valley is still deeply troubled and alienated. Rooting for the Pakistan team against India in a cricket match or raising pro-separatist slogans or demanding *azadi* was and is quite common. The question is not whether those who hold such views are right or wrong. The reality is that they hold those views. The correct response, as we have learnt, is engagement, dialogue and development.

The wrong response is to force hyper-nationalism down the throat of everyone or to bludgeon everyone into accepting a uniform social code of conduct. Four Kashmiri students in Rajasthan were beaten up by other students based on a rumour that they were cooking beef. Why did the police arrest the four students instead of those who beat them up? What business had the police to enter the National Institute of Technology in Srinagar and rain lathi blows on students who were shouting slogans?

We should be concerned that the fires that were lit in Dadri and

JNU have become one and have reached Srinagar. Every attempt is being made by the ultra-nationalists to fan those fires. That path will certainly lead to more violence.

The project of building a Union of States will reach its culmination when the people of the three regions of J&K feel they are truly a part of India. It is a long-term project that can be accomplished only through accommodation and not imposition, through opportunities for participation and not hyper-nationalism, and through innovative federal solutions and not obstinate uniform prescriptions.

KASHMIR IS MORE THAN LAND, IT IS PEOPLE

17 July 2016

I am not surprised that the Kashmir valley is on the boil. The surprise is that it has taken so many months after the demise of Mufti Mohammad Sayeed for the people to rise in revolt.

We must define 'Kashmir'. To most people, it is another state that is part of the territory of India. It may have acceded to India two months after India became independent on 15 August 1947, yet it is an integral part of India. Words are pregnant with meaning: State, territory of India, and integral part of India. The emphasis is on the land.

To some others (a discerning minority), Kashmir is the people of the Kashmir valley, all seven million of them. They acknowledge the unique history of Kashmir and the unique circumstances under which Kashmir acceded to India. The uniqueness was acknowledged by including Article 370 in the Constitution of India. The emphasis is on the people.

The Myopic View

For many years—and even now—governments in Delhi have taken a myopic view that the problem concerns the land (called Kashmir) and hence the land must be defended at all costs. Anything that appears to question the Indian government's sovereignty over the land would not be tolerated. India's sovereignty will be asserted, and defended, by massing troops and police forces on the land. The security forces will be given a legal shield through laws like AFSPA.

That is a legitimate view. It is a view shared by many political parties (with some variations). It is also the view of the defence and other security forces.

Nevertheless, that view is a myopic view. It has not brought us closer to a solution. The distance between the people of Kashmir and the rest of India has only increased over the years. While affirming that J&K, including the Kashmir valley, is a part of India, we must acknowledge that the core of the problem of Kashmir is not land, but the people who live in the Kashmir valley.

Azadi Has Many Meanings

What do the people of Kashmir valley want? When UPA II was in government, we took an all-party delegation to J&K. We spent two days and spent over 16 hours meeting hundreds of people from all walks of life—politicians, academics, students, youth leaders, civil society organisations and many individuals. Many of them uttered the word *azadi*, but the meaning of that word was different to different people. It meant different things like self-determination, independence, autonomy, self-government or devolution of powers. Almost no one openly advocated seceding from India and becoming a part of Pakistan.

What one college student told us is imprinted in my memory. She wanted *azadi* and said 'Remove the security forces'. We asked her 'To where?' Without hesitation she said, 'To the India–Pakistan border'. So, what is her idea of *azadi*? She believes—and it is implicit in her answer—that J&K is a part of India and that the India–Pakistan border must be defended by the forces, but she finds the overpowering presence of security forces oppressive, humiliating and unacceptable.

That is the impression most visitors to J&K carry with them. J&K, and particularly the Kashmir valley, looks like an occupied territory. The people think that successive governments in Delhi did not trust the people of Kashmir. Two years of hyper-nationalist rhetoric, bans prompted by majoritarian viewpoints, and polarisation on the basis of religion have only deepened the distrust.

Mufti Mohammad Sayeed was a reassuring presence and he could have bridged the trust deficit between Kashmir and the Government of India (and the rest of India). He blotted his record by forming a coalition with the BJP but, at least as long he was alive, there was a person with the stature and the moral authority to calm the agitated youth. Alas, he has passed on, the Peoples Democratic Party (PDP)–BJP coalition is limping along without a vision or direction, there is a recrudescence of terrorist incidents, and the youth of Kashmir have erupted in protest against what they perceive to be oppression and excessive use of force. It is back to the 1990s; it is certainly back to the difficult year, 2010, faced by UPA II and the government led by Mr Omar Abdullah.

Gains Lost, Way Forward?

The positive impact of the thinning of security forces and of the splendid work done by the three-member interlocutors group has been nearly completely wiped out. All the gains made during 2011–2015 have been cancelled by the events since January 2016.

Read this assessment by a long-time observer of the Kashmir situation:

'Young Kashmiris are angry about the soldiers constantly in their midst, about the AFSPA, which confers the power to kill with impunity. They want real political change, not the usual suspects who have held the levers of power for far too long. They want business opportunities, not tens of thousands of crores in generous but not job-creating government spending. They want water not oil on the fire.'

Mr Chaitanya Kalbag, the author, is not opposed to the BJP or the government. His warning is prescient and points to what needs to be done. Many people feel the same way but, unfortunately, not those who are in power. Read this comment by Mr Ram Madhav, a BJP strategist and pointsman for J&K: 'Government will stand firm, eruption or no eruption.' Mr Ram Madhav represents those who think that the land of Kashmir must be defended. Mr Chaitanya Kalbag represents those who think that the people of Kashmir must be won over. Between these viewpoints lies the tragedy of Kashmir.

DEFEND THE LAND, WIN OVER THE PEOPLE

24 July 2016

The protests in the Kashmir valley continue for the third week. There is curfew in many parts of the valley. Fresh incidents occur in the valley every day. That is why I have decided to stay with the subject and write a follow-up column to my previous column (*The Indian Express*, 17 July 2016).

During the debate in Parliament last week, many members acknowledged that Kashmir is more than land, it is people. We have, therefore, a good starting point, but we must not walk on the road that we took over the last 40 years.

Asymmetric Distribution

The State of J&K acceded to India in 1947 under a 'grand bargain'. The fundamental premise of the Instrument of Accession dated 26 October 1947 was that J&K will accede to the Dominion of India (and later the Union of India under a new Constitution) on the basis of a special dispensation regarding distribution of powers between the Union and the State of J&K. Article 370 of the Constitution, adopted in 1950, embodied that grand bargain.

In a federal system, it is not unprecedented to have an asymmetric distribution of powers between the Union on the one hand and different states on the other. One state may enjoy special or additional powers. It is precisely this principle that India has advocated in respect of devolution of powers to the Tamil-dominated North and East provinces of Sri Lanka. It is this principle that will be pressed into service while concluding an agreement on the Nagaland issue.

The overwhelming opinion in the Kashmir valley is that Article 370 was honoured in the breach and that the autonomy promised to J&K has been chipped away from time to time. The cry of *azadi* is a response to this perception. Militancy is another. We unequivocally reject militancy and vow to put it down with the power of the State. But is that a reason to equate the cry of *azadi* with militancy? Is that a reason to label every young man or woman who raises the slogan as an anti-national? Is that a reason to regard every speech as seditious?

Honour the Grand Bargain

No one is demanding or advocating a rollback to 1947. Not all events and changes of the last 65 years need to be reversed. Not all the laws that were extended to J&K need to be withdrawn. Many of the changes will be acceptable to the people of J&K as beneficial to them. Many of the laws will be acceptable to them because they are based on universal principles and the replacement laws will not be different.

Besides, the technology-driven changes are irreversible and no one in his right mind will demand a reversal. Take telecommunications. The people of J&K will welcome the fact that they are connected to the rest of India and the world. Other examples are the railways, aviation, power grid, tertiary healthcare, the immunisation programme and skill development, and the laws applicable to the implementation of these schemes and programmes.

As long as J&K remains an integral part of the Union of India, there is ample political and legal space to try out new ideas that will reassure the people of J&K that the Government of India will honour the grand bargain of the accession.

There are other steps that can be taken to retrieve the ground that has been lost since the advent of the PDP–BJP government, but this requires courage—the kind of courage demonstrated by Dr Manmohan Singh when he negotiated with General Musharraf, and by Mr A.B. Vajpayee when he proclaimed that talks can be held under the principle of *insaaniyat.*

Summon Courage

Prime Minister Narendra Modi won a huge popular mandate in 2014. His government enjoys an absolute majority in the Lok Sabha. He has the capacity to take independent decisions without being constrained by his party or his cabinet. Here is a list of things he can do:

1. Withdraw AFSPA from a number of areas immediately.
2. Amend AFSPA in the current session of Parliament. A draft Bill is ready. Start work on repealing AFSPA and replacing it with a reasonable law that will give limited immunity to the Armed Forces.
3. Send an all-party delegation to J&K to meet with all sections of the people and listen to their views. Keep the 'majoritarians' out of the delegation.
4. Direct the Ministry of Defence to draw up a plan (within 15 days) to withdraw as many troops as possible from civilian areas and redeploy the troops closer to the border. Direct them to draw up another plan (within 30 days) for gradually thinning the presence of the Army in the interior (inhabited) areas of J&K.
5. Hand over primary responsibility for maintaining law and order to the state government and the J&K police.
6. Revisit the Standard Operating Procedures for deployment of the security forces, correct the deviations and plug all loopholes.
7. Resurrect the report of the group of interlocutors. Ask Mr Dileep Padgaonkar to update it within 30 days. Set up an empowered group to implement the recommendations.
8. Anything else that appeals to the imagination of the Prime Minister as a step that will not only defend the land but also win over the people of J&K.

We have to travel on a long road and we must begin the journey today.

GAME PLAN, GAMBIT OR GAMBLE?

21 August 2016

As I write this, the curfew in the Kashmir valley has entered the 42nd day. The official death toll of protesters and civilians is 65. The number of security personnel killed is two, not counting the brave men who were killed in encounters with infiltrators. The state government is paralysed, the coalition partners are divided, and the Chief Minister is a hapless spectator: the shots are being called from Delhi.

Several editorial writers and columnists have repeated a phrase that I had used in a statement on 17 August 2016—that J&K is 'sliding into chaos'. The death of Burhan Wani on 8 July 2016 was only the immediate trigger of the slide; the seeds were sown many months ago.

Result Misinterpreted

The election to the J&K Legislative Assembly in 2014 yielded the following result:

PDP:	28
BJP:	25
National Conference (NC):	15
INC:	12
Others:	07
TOTAL:	87

The result was interpreted to mean that the voters wanted the PDP and the BJP to work together and form a government. That was a gross misinterpretation. The electorate wanted the PDP *or* the BJP to form the government and wanted the other party to sit in the Opposition. The PDP could have joined hands with the Congress (they had done it before), or the BJP could have renewed its ties with the NC (Mr Omar Abdullah was a minister in Mr Vajpayee's government). Neither option appears to have been explored seriously. So, it was the default option of a PDP–BJP coalition government.

Issues Intermingled

In the last six weeks, the following issues have become hopelessly intermingled and sane discourse has taken a back seat:

- that India must—and will—defend its border with full force and the security forces will kill or repulse infiltrators;
- that India will not allow Pakistan to meddle in the internal affairs of India, nor allow Pakistan to internationalise the issue of Kashmir;
- that the central government and the J&K government owe a duty to find a solution to the issues raised by the people of J&K (including the issue of displaced Kashmir Pandits) through engagement, discussion and negotiation.

We salute the brave young men who have made the supreme sacrifice while defending the territorial integrity of India. What is debatable is whether the Army should be asked to do more, for example, take primary responsibility for maintaining law and order within the state. Nor can another important debate be circumvented: what is the political solution to the Kashmir issue where thousands of young men and women have poured out on to the streets to protest against perceived injustice?

The central government and the BJP have—the PDP remaining, by choice, a spectator—sought to stifle debate on these issues through raw hyper-nationalistic rhetoric, equating protesters with militants, paternalistic appeals to the 'children', and, everything else failing, abuses and threats to those who have a different point of view.

Last week, the Prime Minister brought in a totally new issue—meddle in the internal affairs of another country—that is certain to muddy the waters further. There are two aspects to the issue of Balochistan: the protest movement in that province and the violation of human rights. India's positions on the two aspects have been clear: the protest movement is an internal matter of Pakistan; India has not played any role in the protests. As far as human rights are concerned, India will highlight the violations in appropriate forums. That was the policy of the governments of Mr Vajpayee and Dr Manmohan Singh.

Brave New World?

That policy was changed last week. At a meeting on 12 August, and in his Independence Day address, Prime Minister Modi announced a new policy that, in effect, meant that if India noticed violation of human rights in Pakistan, it reserved its right to meddle in the affairs of Pakistan. According to some BJP leaders, Modi has opened the door to a brave new world!

Has he? Undoubtedly, Mr Modi chose the occasion carefully, so that it would have the maximum visibility. I doubt, however, if the Prime Minister had weighed the consequences of his words.

The carefully cultivated stance of studied indifference has been jettisoned. Whether India had, or has, a role in the protests in Balochistan will never be known because India had the cover of 'deniability'; that cover has been blown. Pakistan has been virtually invited to meddle in the internal affairs of India on the ground that there are human rights violations in India—the atrocities on Dalits, the threats to Muslims and their food habits, gender violence, child marriages, etc.

The mere mention of Balochistan in a joint statement issued on 16 July 2009 by the Prime Ministers of India and Pakistan was enough to unleash a vitriolic attack by the BJP on Dr Manmohan Singh. Sample: 'The waters of the seven seas will not be able to wash the shame.' From inviting the Prime Minister of Pakistan to the swearing-in on 26 May

2014 to warning Pakistan on the unrest in Balochistan, India's policy on Pakistan has done many U-turns and somersaults worthy of an Olympic medal-winning gymnast.

Sane voices have spoken through editorials and columns. There is a raging fire in our backyard in Kashmir. We must focus on putting out that fire rather than rejoice in the fire in our neighbour's backyard.

WHY NOT TRY AN ALTERNATIVE APPROACH?

18 September 2016

I am sure the Home Minister meant well when he said that he expected the situation in the Kashmir valley to return to normal soon, but it has not and there are no signs it will. The Home Secretary was sending a message of support to the security forces when he said that the situation was improving, but it is not and there are no signs it will.

The Northern Army Commander was pointing the way forward when he said that the government should talk to all stakeholders, but it is common knowledge that the government does not include the separatists (Mr Geelani et al.) in its definition of 'stakeholders'. Mr Ghulam Nabi Azad allowed sufficient space to the government when he said that it is for the government to specify who the stakeholders are, but it is pretty clear that the government has rebuffed the offer to support the government if it enlarged the definition of stakeholders.

Drastic Change in Situation

An all-party delegation went to J&K to the coldest reception in memory. No one came forward to meet the delegation, except the local units of the political parties that were part of the delegation. No chamber of commerce, no non-government organisation, no student body, no trade or employees union, no association of professionals such as lawyers or doctors, no eminent citizen—practically nobody—was willing to meet the delegation. This was in sharp contrast to the huge number of persons and organisations that met a similar delegation in 2010.

Clearly, things have changed between 2010 and 2016. In fact, there has been a drastic change in the situation between 2015 and 2016. The normalcy that had, by and large, returned in 2010 endured until 2014 and continued after the National Democratic Alliance (NDA) government was formed at the Centre. It continued until 1 March 2015, when the PDP–BJP coalition government was formed in J&K under Mufti Mohammad Sayeed. There were great expectations of the new government, but there were also grave apprehensions.

How rapidly the situation in the Kashmir valley has deteriorated since 8 July 2016 has been well chronicled. Why the situation deteriorated so rapidly is a matter of debate. Let me keep that debate aside for the present and focus on the possible solutions.

More of the Same...

One possible solution is to continue with the same approach as before: place the responsibility for internal security in the hands of the Army and the central armed police forces, continue with the AFSPA, send more forces to the valley, impose curfew, shun the separatist leaders and detain them if necessary, apprehend the 'leaders' of the agitation, use force to quell protests and blame Pakistan for instigating the protests in the valley. In short, administer the same medicine (it hasn't worked so far) in the hope that it will, in due course, contain and cure the affliction.

Another possible solution is to look at alternative medicine. Allopathy is a great system of medicine, but alternative systems of medicine have also gained wide acceptance. Likewise, why not try an alternative approach to the situation in J&K?

I do not intend to be provocative. I do not challenge the intentions of the governments (past and present). I accept that everyone genuinely desires to find a durable solution. If I indeed provoke, it is to provoke a constructive debate.

...Or Alternative Approach?

Let's begin with **AFSPA**: I have two suggestions. Firstly, announce the repeal of AFSPA, assure the armed forces that AFSPA will be replaced by a more humane law (not leaving a vacuum) and appoint a group to draft a new law quickly. Secondly, withdraw the application of AFSPA from select areas as an experimental measure.

Deployment: Instead of sending more troops to the valley, withdraw some units from the populated areas of the valley and send them to the border to strengthen the defence against infiltrators and potential terrorists. Send the message that the government trusts the people not to violate law and order.

Governance: Retrieve the report of the interlocutors appointed in 2010. There are many suggestions and proposals that can be implemented without opposition from any quarter. Identify them and begin their implementation.

Reiterate the stand of the Northern Army Commander: Appoint a small group of interlocutors to begin talks forthwith with stakeholders. It will take time, patience and persuasion but, eventually, different groups of stakeholders will come forward to meet the group of interlocutors.

Review of laws: Many laws were extended to J&K. Such extension is considered by the vast majority of the people of the state as unwarranted and in breach of the Instrument of Accession as well as Article 370 of the Constitution. So, why not ask the state legislature to do a comprehensive review of the extended laws and make laws on the subjects where it feels state legislation will suffice? Nothing will be lost if the state legislature makes laws to replace the

- Advocates Welfare Fund Act,
- Apartment Ownership Act,
- Ayurvedic and Unani Practitioners Act,
- ....,
- ....,

- Wakfs Act,
- Water Supply Act and so on.

Most of these can be replaced by state legislation. Our fears about state autonomy in legislation are grossly exaggerated.

Given a fair trial, the alternative approach may work like alternative medicine. If nothing, it will bridge the present, and rapidly widening, trust deficit between the people of the Kashmir valley and the governments (at the Centre and in the state).

MISADVENTURES AND MISGOVERNANCE

There are many seemingly unrelated columns in this section. The common thread that runs through them is that each column highlights an issue that concerns governance or, more accurately, is an example of misgovernance. I wrote two columns on the state of the judiciary. While the judiciary is eager to correct the errors and the excesses of the legislature and the executive, it has proven incapable of addressing its own shortcomings. As the vacancies in courts and the backlog of cases pile up, the justice-delivery system is facing a near collapse. In another column, I listed the misadventures of the government that are also examples of misgovernance.

NEW YEAR RESOLUTIONS FOR THE NDA GOVERNMENT

3 January 2016

I don't like making New Year's resolutions, but I am happy to make resolutions for others in the sure belief that they will be broken before the week is over. There is no fun in making resolutions for the poor, the meek or the peacemakers. It is better to make resolutions for the high and mighty, and watch the fun while they break them. Who or what is the most omnipresent, omnipotent and omniscient entity in the country today? Undoubtedly, the Modi government, or so it is believed by a cross-section of the people, especially those who wear bespoken suits, the media, the 281 elected + 2 (nominated) MPs of the Lok Sabha, the happy family called the Sangh Parivar, the *swayamsevaks* and the never-say-die *bhakts*. So, indulge me, while I propose some New Year's resolutions for the government of Mr Narendra Modi.

1. We shall impress upon the Prime Minister that he should visit different parts of India, a country just as lovely as the United States or France or China or Japan or Fiji, and address the people of India who are just as friendly as the *bhaiyon aur behnon*[1] who had gathered in large

[1]Brothers and sisters

numbers at the Madison Square garden or the Wembley stadium. We believe that the 31 per cent of the resident voters who voted for the NDA are entitled to see and hear the Prime Minister as much as the non-resident potential voters.

2. We shall read the Riot Act to the compulsive talkers in the government and the party and issue an order that they shall forthwith stop unburdening themselves of their pet theories and edicts. If they cannot, then, they shall do so only in one of two languages—Prakrit or Pali—and no translations shall be issued to the media.

For the Economy

1. We shall temper expectations—and estimates—of GDP growth in small steps. We erred in taking a giant leap from the original estimate of 8.5 per cent in January 2015 to 7.3 per cent in December 2015. Small steps are less noticed. A small step for the Finance Minister is a giant step for the economy.
2. We shall do a mutual change of positions between Dr Raghuram Rajan and Dr Arvind Subramanian. That will allow Dr Subramanian, the Governor of the RBI, to cut the interest rate (his long-cherished desire) and Dr Rajan, the CEA, to cut the fiscal deficit (his long-cherished desire).

For Good Governance

1. We shall revise the charters of the main agencies. The CBI will be the new National Consumer Disputes Redressal Commission (NCDRC); the Intelligence Bureau (IB) will be the new Press Information Bureau (PIB); and the Serious Frauds Investigation Office (SFIO) will be the new Board of Control for Cricket in India (BCCI). The charters of other agencies will be revised after due consultation with the RSS.
2. We shall adopt the slogan *Chalo chalein Amit Shah ke saath* in the five state Assembly elections of 2016. Since we do not expect to win

in any of the five, we don't have to project anyone as chief minister. God unwilling, suppose we win, we shall appoint Mr Amit Shah as the chief minister of that state.

For Our Friends and Unfriends

1. We shall promulgate an ordinance to permit cricket associations (especially Rajasthan Cricket Association [RCA]) to have their offices and hold meetings of their executive committee and general body outside India. This will enable Mr Lalit Modi to attend meetings of the RCA on compassionate grounds and disable the Enforcement Directorate (ED) from searching the venue.
2. We shall restore the position of a sole municipal corporation for Delhi and vest in the Municipal Corporation of Delhi (MCD) all the powers now assigned to the government of the Union Territory. Between two evenly-empowered functionaries (the Lieutenant Governor and the Mayor), Mr Arvind Kejriwal will be the odd man. We shall reserve the right to proclaim martial law in Delhi and to appoint the Police Commissioner as the martial law administrator (mainly to control the traffic, pollution and commissions of enquiry).
3. We shall persuade the Prime Minister to grant a free-wheeling interview to the Times Now channel with one change—the interview will be done by the Jain brothers, who own the channel. The nation and the Jain brothers want to know what the Prime Minister thinks of Mr Arnab Goswami.
4. We shall finally carry out the long-promised cabinet reshuffle: The new portfolios of the top four (who cannot be moved out of North or South Blocks) will be: Mr Rajnath Singh, Finance Minister; Ms Sushma Swaraj, Home Minister; Mr Arun Jaitley, Defence Minister; and Mr Manohar Parrikar, External Affairs Minister. So, instead of square pegs in round holes, we will have round pegs in square holes.

Happy New Year!

CROUCHING TIGER VS HIDDEN DRAGON

14 February 2016

How quickly an idea or a word or a phrase can spread across a country! In a matter of weeks, the phrase 'net neutrality' went from a term used by a small group of tech industry insiders and academics to a phrase of common usage. The phrase means that the Internet will treat all content it carries equally, indifferent to the nature of the content or the identity of the user.

It was as if there was an election. There was a high decibel campaign between 9 December 2015 and 8 February 2016. There were two parties. In a sense, there was voting, where people were asked to respond to a consultation paper put out by the Telecom Regulatory Authority of India (TRAI). The only thing missing were the election symbols. Crouching Tiger and Hidden Dragon would have been apt symbols for the two sides.

The hidden dragon argued for allowing service providers to be able to give free access to certain websites and to price access to other content differently. The face of the campaign on this side was Facebook and its founder, Mr Mark Zuckerberg. The crouching tiger argued for net neutrality. There was no identified face on this side, but there was National Association of Software and Services Companies (NASSCOM), there were many passionate individuals, and there was a hashtag #SavetheInternet. The government was a silent, but somewhat wary, player.

Net Neutrality Wins

Had it not been for the citizens' movement, the net neutrality consultation held by TRAI may have ended differently. TRAI and the government made confusing noises last year. The consultation paper on over-the-top services sent mixed signals. Initially, the government did not make any commitment to protect net neutrality. When a committee of the Department of Telecommunications supported net neutrality, the Ministry of Communications did not fully own the committee's view. However, when TRAI published the Regulations on 8 February, net neutrality was the winner.

The Regulations are categorical: 'No service provider shall offer or charge discriminatory tariffs for data services on the basis of content.' They also prohibit service providers from entering into agreements with any person that could lead to discriminatory tariffs. The only exceptions will be content related to some emergency services and closed electronic communication networks.

Rival Arguments

Common protocols bind the Internet as a network of networks. In the early 1980s, the pioneers of Internet sent a tough command that required everyone to implement common protocols or risk going off the Internet. That fiat enabled the open nature of the network and laid the foundations for the Internet's rapid growth. If service providers get to slice and package Internet content, this principle would be compromised, and they would have excessive power to influence consumer behaviour. This is especially relevant in the case of persons who have never used the Internet before. On the other hand, those who favour giving service providers freedom to package and price content differently make the 'free market' argument—let them provide the service in any way they want, and competition will take care of everything. They also argue that free access to the Internet will lead to inclusion of those—two out of three Indians today—who do not have access. They point to the United

States (US) and many countries of Europe that have not opted for a blanket ban on differential pricing, and to many countries who have not yet taken any regulatory decision.

Classification vs Discrimination

TRAI has recognised that restricted access is not a solution and also that inclusion does not mean poor quality access for poor people. But is the debate settled finally? I doubt it.

There are two, if not more, hurdles. The first is because TRAI does not have the final word. Its decision can be appealed to the Telecom Disputes Settlement Appellate Tribunal (TDSAT). Its regulations can also be challenged in the High Court and the Supreme Court, and in all probability they will be. The second hurdle is the Constitution of India. TRAI has equated 'differential tariffs' with 'discriminatory tariffs'. The Constitution permits classification based on intelligible differentia. A case of permissible 'classification' will not be a case of impermissible 'discrimination'. Suppose a user has no interest in any content except limited content (contained in certain websites). Can't a service provider offer a package of content that would be directly useful to a farmer or a student or a homemaker, justify that package as a separate class of content, and offer it for free to the user in order to retain the custom of the user? TRAI has not addressed this question.

Debate Not Over

I broadly support TRAI's decision. My worry, however, is that the regulations are too definitive and categorical and allow no room for innovation or experimentation. The US and some European countries allow or disallow models on a case-by-case basis.

The full consequences of TRAI's blanket ban will play out in the months and years to come and I hope that, in due course, TRAI would amend the regulations suitably to allow for exceptions in public interest. Net neutrality is not a slogan and regulations are not slogans written into the law; they need to have more nuance. Net neutrality is a larger concept than the differential pricing issue addressed in the new regulations. India may need a parliamentary law on the subject. The debate and the policy-making process on net neutrality are far from over.

GOVERNMENT SHOULD BACK CJI ON THE IDEA OF A COURT OF APPEAL

1 May 2016

The subject cannot be dealt within a single column; nevertheless I think I should make a beginning.

The breakdown of the justice-delivery system is happening before our eyes. Ask any judge of any court or ask any lawyer, and they will tell you that it is only pretence that is keeping a smile on the faces of judges.

The numbers tell the story. Against 1,065 approved posts of judges in the High Courts, only 633 judges are in place. In the subordinate courts, there are 4,432 vacancies (in 20,502 posts). Pendency of cases at different levels was:

- Subordinate courts: 26,488,405 (December 2014)
- High Courts: 4,153,957 (December 2014)
- Supreme Court: 59,468 (February 2016)

Insufficient Judges, Unwilling Lawyers

The problems of the justice-delivery system have been discussed, debated and dissected so many times, and in so many reports, that if anyone suggests another 'study' before some obvious reforms are done, he deserves to be shot! The core of the problem is that we have too few judges: just 12 judges per million population. We need more judges. The demand is there, but where is the supply? On top of that we have a system of judges appointing judges that, in the view of some, has turned the constitutional provision on its head. The result: there is vehement disagreement between the judiciary on the one hand, and the executive/Parliament on the other, on the manner of appointment of judges.

Few able and successful lawyers are ready to accept judgeship. The only sure source of recruitment to the High Court is from the rank of District Judge, but long years in the lower judiciary leave very few unscathed by truth or allegations. In desperation, a certain number of judges have been appointed from time to time, but the quality of appointments has been uneven.

The justice-delivery system requires a root and branch reform. We can start anywhere, but if we want quick and visible results it is better to start at the top. That is why the proposal for a National Judicial Appointments Commission (NJAC) and the new proposal for a National Court of Appeal (a level between the High Courts and the Supreme Court) have gained traction.

Appellate Jurisdiction

Why a Court of Appeal? For a number of reasons—insufficient number of judges, workload, proliferation of laws, complex disputes, new jurisdictions, etc.—the quality of judgements delivered by the High Courts is not high or even. More and more judgements and orders are appealed against. In the case of new jurisdictions conferred on the High Courts, there is a genuine need to provide one court of appeal both on facts and law. Today, appeals from the High Courts as well as from various Appellate Tribunals land up in the Supreme Court. The earlier restraints of seeking a certificate or leave to appeal from the High Court have been done away with. Article 136 of the Constitution, which is strictly a provision to seek *special* leave to appeal, has virtually become a regular provision for appeal. The only gatekeeper is the Supreme Court, which dismisses most special leave petitions (SLPs) at the stage of admission, but it has to necessarily hear the case before it dismisses it. As a result, the docket keeps growing; so does the backlog; and the Supreme Court has become a court of correction. The judges have no choice but to sit in benches of two judges.

If the status of the Supreme Court must be restored to that of a truly Constitutional Court, it must shed most of the work it does now—and create another competent forum that will take over that work. Hence, the case for a Court of Appeal. Nearly 80 per cent of the SLPs now heard by the Supreme Court—pleas for bail, for eviction or protection from eviction, for appointment of arbitrators; appeals from criminal cases or civil suits or interim orders; service, labour, matrimonial and land acquisition cases, etc.—can be heard by the Court of Appeal, and the outcome will be just as satisfactory as a judgement rendered by the Supreme Court.

We have enough distinguished judges in the High Courts who can be appointed to the Court of Appeal until they attain the age of 65—same as a Supreme Court judge. Five regional benches of the Court of Appeal will require about 40 judges and they will be happy and proud to serve for three more years.

Restore Constitutional Court

This will also pave the way for reform of the Supreme Court. A smaller court with no more than 20 outstanding jurist-judges; deeper selection from among judges, jurists and senior lawyers; benches of not less than three judges; the Constitution Bench as a regular feature; more time devoted to a case; quicker disposal; and well-considered judgements that will declare the law for the whole country will be some of the benefits that will accrue, thanks to the reform.

Concurrently, the issue of the NJAC should be resolved, paving the way for appointment of the best available talent to the higher judiciary.

The Chief Justice of India (CJI) proposed the idea of a Court of Appeal, but I was dismayed when the government, too quickly and abruptly, shot it down. I hope the idea is still alive and will be debated. In addressing the complex matter of delivery of justice, the idea would be a beginning of the end of an over-burdened and choked Supreme Court and the restoration of a true Constitutional Court. Other reforms should follow quickly.

MISADVENTURES OF THE MODI GOVERNMENT

15 May 2016

Back in the summer of 2014, almost anything was possible for the BJP government. The once-in-a-generation mandate had endowed the government with enormous political capital that could be used to implement any reform, including some long-pending and difficult reforms. Alas, two years after May 2014, the government has become a punchline for jokes.

Its hard-core supporters are scrambling desperately to defend it. Many who had voted for the BJP are looking for alternatives, as they did in the elections in Delhi and Bihar. The government's political capital has depleted considerably.

One of the main reasons for the turnabout is the government's tendency to embark upon expensive misadventures. A party that showed considerable political skill in winning the general election has made some inexplicably strange miscalculations since it came to power. Here are some examples:

Legislative Misadventures

Amendments to the Land Acquisition Act: Amendments to the Right to Fair Compensation and Transparency in Land Acquisition, Rehabilitation and Resettlement Act, 2013, were sought to be pushed through without due consultations with stakeholders. It made no sense to amend crucial sections of the Act so soon after it was passed with the BJP's support. After promulgating an ordinance more than once, the government finally gave up.

GST Bill: The government tried to bulldoze the Opposition into supporting a flawed GST Constitution Amendment Bill. It has obstinately refused to engage in a dialogue with the Congress on the latter's reasoned points of difference. Result: the GST Bill is yet to be passed and more doubts about the Bill are being expressed with every passing day.

Aadhaar Bill: It was not a Money Bill, yet the Speaker was persuaded to declare it as a Money Bill so that it could navigate the choppy waters of the Rajya Sabha. It was a stupid ploy and, as could be expected, the faux Money Bill has been challenged before the Supreme Court. It is possible that another shipwreck is a few weeks away.

Target the Congress

Congress Mukt Bharat Mission: It was, and always will be, a mission impossible, yet the Modi–Shah combine decided to give it top priority. The prime target was the Nehru–Gandhi family. Other targets were also selected. Cases were manufactured, pliant officers were placed in the investigating agencies, innuendoes and leaks became the order of the day, and sections of the media were suborned to do the dirty work of the government. The misadventure has made all Opposition parties more suspicious and ruined what little chance there was to cobble support for the passage of selected Bills or implementation of vital administrative reforms. Is there today one political party (including the Shiv Sena) or one state government (including the Biju Janata Dal [BJD] government in Odisha) that is willing to trust the central government?

Pseudo-nationalism: Starting with the bogus sedition case against a bunch of JNU students based on a doctored video, the government launched a nationwide campaign to create the perception of an 'enemy within'. The only thing this strategy seems to have achieved is to turn college campuses from Hyderabad to Pune to Aligarh to Jadavpur into war zones. Add to that the stoking of divisive fires like 'ban beef', 'say *Bharat Mata ki Jai*', 'kill rationalists', etc., and the stage is set for deeper polarisation and the ghettoisation of towns and cities. Equating nationalism with Hindutva and a right-wing, atavistic agenda is the final blow to *Sabka Saath Sabka Vikas*.

Attempts to topple governments: The crude attempt to topple the Uttarakhand government has failed miserably, leaving the central government licking its wounds. Sadly, the President has been embarrassed because he was advised to sign the Proclamation near midnight when the trust vote was fixed for 11 a.m. the next day. All political parties are suspicious that the BJP will not allow space for any other political party.

Clean chit to terror accused: The portents are ominous. The procession of witnesses turning hostile has begun in the Samjhauta and Ajmer *dargah* cases. A prosecutor spilled the beans when she said that she had been advised to 'go slow'. Charge sheets are being revised, notably in the Malegaon blast case. The most startling statement was made by the Director General of the National Investigation Agency (NIA) who, when asked about right-wing terror, told *The Week* magazine that 'since 2008, there has been no activity that has come to the notice of the agency. Hence, there is no question of any threat'. It was a command performance.

Absent, a Foreign Policy

Nepal: Whatever the government might say, the perception in Nepal is that India continues to interfere in the internal affairs of Nepal. The latest accusation is of a conspiracy to topple the Oli government. A key neighbour is more alienated now than at any time in memory.

Pakistan: If flip-flop can be called policy, India does have a Pakistan policy! Nothing could have been more naive than inviting a joint investigation team (JIT) from Pakistan to 'investigate' the terrorist attack on the Pathankot Air Force Station. The JIT played its role to perfection and, on returning home, trashed the evidence given by the Indian side and gave a clean chit to Pakistan's State and non-State actors. It was an international embarrassment.

China: The recent visa episodes exposed the bumbling Ministry of Home Affairs and the fumbling Ministry of External Affairs. They were just the latest in a long series of foreign policy misadventures that have ended in ignominious retreats by the government.

No adventure is without a cost. The biggest cost is in terms of what could have been achieved, in both consensus-building and development, had the government chosen a wiser path on each of these matters.

SILENCE—THE NEW GOLD STANDARD OF GOVERNANCE

31 July 2016

India elected an eloquent, some would say voluble, candidate as Prime Minister. Prime Minister Narendra Modi speaks frequently, tweets extensively and writes sparingly. No one is surprised when he seizes the occasion and speaks. It is only when he ignores the occasion and withdraws into silence that questions are raised. Here are a few samples of his silence:

VYAPAM: That is the acronym for the Professional Examination Board in Madhya Pradesh where a BJP government has been in office since 2003. Examinations were fixed for many years. The scandal was exposed in 2013 by a whistle-blower. After many legal battles, the case was transferred to the CBI. Meanwhile, 40 persons connected with the case (witnesses, investigating officers, accused) have met with unnatural deaths. Whistle-blowers and activists have received multiple threats. In any other case, the scandal would have unseated the Chief Minister, but Mr Shivraj Singh Chouhan's government survives. The Prime Minister is the silent fox. It is his silence that keeps Mr Chouhan in office.

Lalit Modi: He is the former boss of the Indian Premier League (IPL) and is wanted in India for questioning. He fled to the UK where a friendly government bent the rules to give him refuge (even while hundreds of

Indians who do not hold a valid passport are routinely deported). The Chief Minister of Rajasthan endorsed Mr Lalit Modi's plea for being allowed to stay in the UK and requested that her letter may not be disclosed to the Indian authorities. The External Affairs Minister supported his case for a UK travel document after her Ministry cancelled his passport. Mr Lalit Modi thumbs his nose at the Indian investigative agencies and holidays around the world travelling on a UK passport. The Prime Minister is the silent saviour of his Minister and the Chief Minister.

Wages of Intolerance

Kalburgi, Dabholkar and Pansare: One was an atheist. Another campaigned against superstition. The third portrayed the warrior-king, Shivaji, as a secular ruler. They were murdered, and the investigating agencies suspect there are common features in the three cases. Eminent writers voiced their protest by returning the awards given to them by the Sahitya Akademi. The Prime Minister was unconcerned and maintained a stoic silence. The literary world felt humiliated.

Rohith Vemula: 'My birth is my fatal accident', wrote the Dalit PhD scholar Rohith Vemula, before he took his own life. Campuses erupted in protest. It turned into a familiar battle between the 'entitled' and the 'disentitled'. The central government tried to prove that Rohith was not a Dalit. No one, so far, has been held responsible or accountable for his death. The Prime Minister remained a silent spectator. The disentitled are gripped by fear.

Akhlaq: Akhlaq was lynched by a mob who believed that he had stored beef in his home. A bizarre enquiry was launched, not into the lynching, but into the nature of the animal meat! Political leaders spoke in favour of the mob, communal tensions were aroused, and the Prime Minister's studied silence invited comment. When he appeared to have decided to break his silence, it was only to deliver a homily on how Hindus and Muslims should fight poverty and not each other. On Akhlaq's killing, he has maintained a studied silence.

Clumsy Manoeuvres

JNU: Suddenly, it was discovered that JNU was filled with anti-nationals. Barring members of the ABVP, every JNU student was presumed to be an anti-national unless he proved his nationalism by raising the slogan '*Bharat Mata ki Jai*'. Police slapped sedition charges on students, lawyers roughed up journalists on the court's premises, the university rusticated student leaders and the Prime Minister erected a wall of silence between himself and the tumult outside.

The Pathankot attack: Barely days after the Prime Minister made an impromptu visit to Prime Minister Nawaz Sharif's home in Lahore, six terrorists attacked the Air Force Station at Pathankot. It was revealed that the government had received intelligence about the threat but mishandled it. The government's clumsy attempt to forge a 'deal' on reciprocal investigation came a cropper. Pakistan sent its team to Pathankot, brazenly denied it got any evidence from the Indian agencies and delivered a lethal snub by rejecting their request for a reciprocal visit to Pakistan. The Prime Minister's response was grave silence.

Atrocities on Dalits: The false promise of *Sabka Saath Sabka Vikas* is unravelling. Atrocities on Dalits are a fact of Indian life. The Una incident exposed the right-wing Hindutva brigade's hypocrisy, exploitation and arrogance. The Prime Minister has observed a silence that is deafening even amidst the uproar.

Duty to Speak

In the 2014 elections, the Indian voter was swayed by the eloquence of Mr Narendra Modi. Not many have cultivated the art of public speaking as Mr Modi has. Is he now cultivating the art of public silence? I readily concede that a Prime Minister is not required to speak on every occasion or on every subject but, when there is a duty to speak, silence is unacceptable. Silence can be a strategy, silence can be a tactic, but silence can never be an answer to the ills of our polity and the fault lines of our society. When an eloquent and willing-to-speak Prime Minister deliberately chooses not to speak, decent citizens will be concerned, students will demand answers, Muslims will feel alienated and Dalits will feel threatened. All of those do not augur well.

of the total sanctioned strength of 1,079 judges, only 601 are in place. In many High Courts the proportion of vacant posts is nearly 50 per cent and, in four High Courts, it is over 50 per cent. Every judge is carrying the workload of two judges. Workaholic judges sit up to 6 p.m. on many days. Where is the time to read legal literature, or the time to reflect, or the time to write judgements? In several cases, judgements are reserved and remain pending for more than a year.

The data on pendency is frightening:

- Supreme Court: 62,657 cases
- High Courts: 3,870,373 cases

It will take years to eliminate the backlog—that is, if it can be eliminated at all. The problem of pendency is so humongous that I cannot think of any system of 'case management' that would be able to bring the problem under control. Most judges have, therefore, given up: they discharge their duties conscientiously and dispose of as many cases as possible without worrying about the backlog.

Give Up Subterfuge

As vacancies accumulate, the task of filling those vacancies has become more challenging. If one or two vacancies in a High Court have to be filled every quarter, the task is manageable. If there are 82 vacancies in 160 posts (as in the case of the Allahabad High Court), how do you fill them in one go? How will you sort out issues of inter-se seniority among the lawyer-candidates? How will you ensure that the ratio between candidates from the Bar and the Bench (District Judges) is maintained at 2:1?

The casualty is justice. Cases are adjourned repeatedly. In the Delhi High Court, it is difficult to get the 'next date of hearing' within three-four months; it is no different in other High Courts. Clients have to bear the cost of frequent adjournments (travel, lawyer's fees, etc.). When a case is heard, it cannot be heard continuously. Fresh cases for admission get only a few minutes of hearing. Everyone, including the judges, has a sense of dissatisfaction and disappointment.

The government may be aiming at a 'perfect' MoP in which elements of the NJAC could be incorporated. The government must give up the subterfuge. The only way to assert Parliament's sovereign right—if Parliament wishes to do so—is to enact a new Constitution Amendment Act that will pass muster. Otherwise, the government is obliged to present an MoP that is consistent with the letter and spirit of the judgement.

The standoff between the Collegium and the government is unacceptable because it will only accelerate the collapse of the justice-delivery system.

POLICY FAILURES

Mr Narendra Modi's party is renowned for its U-turns—on MGNREGA, on Aadhaar and on GST. These are only prominent examples, there were many more. Actually, I welcomed these U-turns because they signalled the return of the government to the path of good policy and good governance. Imagine the catastrophic consequences of winding up MGNREGA when large parts of the country had suffered due to two successive years of drought. Or imagine the fallout of scrapping Aadhaar that is now the pillar on which many programmes and schemes of the government stand. The lesson for any government is that there is no merit in rubbishing everything that the previous government conceived or implemented.

PRICE OF PROCRASTINATION

8 January 2016

I write this with a profound sense of grief, contrition and disappointment bordering on despair.

Since the subject I have chosen for this special column is the terrorist attack on the Pathankot Air Force base, I resolved that I should weigh every word and phrase with extra caution before I committed them to paper and ultimately to print.

First, let me salute the valour of the seven men who were killed in the terrorist attack. Five of them were retired and re-employed jawans and, presumably, no longer subjected to training or drill; one was killed despite being highly skilled; and one lost his life while engaging the terrorists. I mourn their deaths along with their families and millions of citizens.

Second, I rue the fact that several internal security tasks remained unfinished when the UPA government demitted office in May 2014, the most important among them being the constitution of the National Counter Terrorism Centre (NCTC). The key pillars of counterterrorism are intelligence, analysis, and single command and control. More often than not, raw information lies as raw information and is practically useless. Honing information into intelligence is called analysis and that is a specialist's function. In the complex world of counterterrorism, high-quality analysis requires a multidisciplinary approach bringing together the skills of the border guard and the computer technologist, the policeman and the professor (of chemistry or engineering or psychology), the spy and the scientist. The third pillar is a single command and control to undertake counterterrorist operations.

I had reflected on the idea of an NCTC for many months. We had engaged with many experts in the field. We had studied different models. I was convinced that the NCTC was an imperative, especially in a federal system with as many police administrations as there are states and Union Territories. We had already made a beginning with the Multi Agency Centre (MAC) within the IB and in every state, and it required only two or three more courageous steps to constitute the NCTC. My feeling of remorse is because I did not succeed in notifying the NCTC before I left the Ministry of Home Affairs on 31 July 2012. It is a long story and shall be told on another day. Suffice for the present to say that the NCTC was stalled by blind and unreasoned opposition.

Fundamental Change

The thousands of words spoken and written in the last few days (though I admit I have not heard or read them all) seem to have missed a fundamental change in the nature of the threat faced by the country today. One of the worst terror attacks on Indian soil took place on the four horror-filled days between 26 and 29 November 2008. Since then, there have been four major terrorist attacks and several minor ones. The major attacks were carried out in Pune, Mumbai, Delhi and Hyderabad. What marked them out as fundamentally different from other major attacks in the past was that there was no proven connection to Pakistan. They were carried out by Indian-born and Indian-bred terrorists. The investigation pointed to the Indian Mujahedeen or Students Islamic Movement of India (SIMI) and, in the case of the Delhi attack, to a Kashmiri group. Likewise, the minor incidents were also traced to Indian groups in different states.

That fundamental difference seems to have vanished since 2015. We seem to be back to the pre-2008 days. The Pakistani State or non-State is back as the source. Terrorist attacks in Dinanagar, district Gurdaspur in

Punjab (27 July 2015), Udhampur in J&K (5 August 2015) and Pathankot in Punjab (2 January 2016) and some minor incidents have been traced back to Pakistan.

Third, my disappointment is with the manner in which the counter-terror system in the government responded to the situation that had fundamentally changed since the middle of 2015. It is a fair inference that the foreign office, the defence forces and the internal security establishment have not noted the change and have not been talking to each other.

No Single Command

My disappointment turned to despair as the nation watched the response to the Pathankot attack. It was *déjà vu*. There was no sign of a 'single command and control'. The Defence Security Corps re-employs retired jawans who are not much better than armed gatekeepers. The Garud Force is a defensive arm of the Air Force to protect Air Force assets. The National Security Guard (NSG) is a target-specific counterterrorist force, not a battlefield unit. Yet, these were the units that were called in as the first responders. The one trained battle-ready counterterrorist force, the Army's Special Forces, was nearby, but not deployed to secure the sprawling base or the perimeter.

Does the Home Minister meet with the NSA, the Home Secretary, the Special Secretary (Internal Security) and the heads of the IB and Research and Analysis Wing (RAW) every day? It appears not. Had MAC provided inputs in the days immediately prior to 1 January? We do not know. Was the cabinet committee on security convened immediately after the security forces engaged the terrorists? There is no official word, but the Home Minister did not attend any meeting after 2 January 2016.

As the saying goes, 'things happen'; but we cannot let things happen. The matter of security of the people cannot be left to individuals, however brilliant they may be. We need an institutional arrangement and the response to a terror attack must be an institutional response led, no doubt, by brilliant individuals.

Is there a case for constituting the NCTC? Look no further than the

Pathankot terror attack. The draft notification was revised after taking into account the states' concerns and sensibilities. The revised draft leaves room for any reluctant state to join the NCTC after an interval of time (as was done in the case of value added tax [VAT]). The draft notification is on the Home Minister's table. A copy is with the Prime Minister's Office (PMO).

The best message of reassurance to a shaken and sceptical nation and the best warning to our enemies that we take terrorism as a serious threat will be to notify forthwith the NCTC.

MGNREGA—MAKING A MEAL OF WORDS

7 February 2016

Parliament is the highest legislative body. The Prime Minister is the Chief Executive of the country. A statement made by the Prime Minister in Parliament must have a certain sanctity and solemnity.

On 27 February 2015, while replying to the debate on the Motion of Thanks to the President's address, Prime Minister Modi said:

'Sometimes, we are told that we will or we are about to discontinue MGNREGA or have closed down MGNREGA… Most of you believe that I have very good political sense. And that political sense does not allow me to discontinue MGNREGA. I cannot make such a mistake because MGNREGA is a living monument of your failures. After 60 years of Independence, people had to dig pits because of you, therefore it is a biggest example of your failures and I am going to propagate this with all my might. I will tell the world that the pits you are digging point towards your wrongdoings of 60 years.' Was it a heartless, political taunt thrown at the Congress? Or was it a conclusion arrived at after deliberation and analysis? It is difficult to say, as with most remarks of Prime Minister Modi. There was genuine apprehension that the rural employment guarantee programme would be allowed to wither away and die.

Tried, but Failed

The government did try to cut back the programme. It delayed releases of funds, and made it difficult for state governments to respond to the demand for work. Evidence of that was strong: the percentage of payment generated within 15 days dropped from 50 in 2013–14 to 26.85 in 2014–15. The person-days of employment that were generated came down sharply, as will be seen from the following:

- 2012–13: 230 crore person-days
- 2013–14: 220 crore
- 2014–15: 166 crore

Consequently, the number of households that completed 100 days of wage employment dropped from more than 51 lakh in 2012–13 to 25 lakh in 2014–15.

The programme that Mr Modi had disparagingly equated with 'digging pits' has just completed 10 years. And who was celebrating the occasion with pomp and enthusiasm? The NDA government! The government is all over the media claiming credit for the programme's success!

The distress situation created by drought this year has meant that the demand for MGNREGA has been huge. The government has even sanctioned 50 additional days of employment in drought-affected areas. It seems the government is beginning to see the good in the scheme. Sadly for the government, it cannot simply rename MGNREGA and appropriate credit. MGNREGA is too well known to be simply renamed.

The Positive Side...

MGNREGA has served as an important shock absorber for the rural economy. Firstly, it provides immediate relief in times of distress and, in that sense, it is automatically counter-cyclical. In times of drought, the demand for work goes up. Secondly, since it works on a self-selection method, there is minimal discretion to choose who gets work. Thirdly, because payment is made directly into bank or post-office accounts, there are fewer leakages in this scheme than in many other welfare schemes. Fourthly, MGNREGA wages have set the floor for wages for casual, manual work—per capita wage in rural India has increased at an average annual rate of 12 per cent over the 10 years up to 2014–15.

The scheme is an important instrument in the larger context of the transformation under way in India. A large number of persons are moving, or have to move, from agriculture to manufacturing or services. Many people first undertake seasonal migration for some time each year before finding opportunities that are more permanent. This means that work must be found back in the village during the months one is without work in urban areas. Besides, for the millions of workers who do not leave the village at all, MGNREGA provides valuable employment during the lean seasons when farm-based employment is low.

...And the Negative

However, there are aspects of the scheme that I have questioned from the very beginning. The 'works' undertaken are usually deepening of water bodies or cutting the overgrowth on road margins. Important as they are, the panchayat should look at the full menu of 'works' that has been expanded to include water conservation, construction and maintenance of irrigation canals, drought-proofing (afforestation), renovation of water bodies, land development, sanitation work, building rural roads, flood control, watershed development, and drinking water. A very wide choice of works has given room for the panchayat (read: the president of the panchayat) to choose the work that is most 'popular' and least 'demanding'. I think we should adopt the exactly opposite approach: require the panchayat to identify the assets that are badly needed in the village and choose the MGNREGA works from among them.

MGNREGA is not a dole programme—money is given against work. Humongous amounts are spent every year as wages. About 10 crore workers are presently active. We should be able to leverage these to create durable, permanent and useful assets.

MGNREGA was never about 'digging pits' nor is it a 'monument to failure'. As Mr Modi has made a meal of his words, the time has come to convert the programme into one that will create 'durable assets' and become a 'monument to social justice'.

AADHAAR BILL—ENDS RIGHT, MEANS WRONG

20 March 2016

History can be told through stories. So can politics. If you wish to explain the politics of India through a story, you need to go no further than the story of Aadhaar.

Aadhaar is a unique identification number that is intended to be given to all Indian residents. The idea is not novel or unprecedented. India was a latecomer to the idea of a unique identity number. I cannot but recall the fierce opposition to the idea. Ms Meenakshi Lekhi called Aadhaar 'a fraud', Mr Prakash Javdekar described it as 'a game played on the poor' and Mr Ananth Kumar said it was 'something to be ashamed of'. Now, the BJP is the champion of Aadhaar and has piloted a controversial Bill through both the Houses of Parliament! That success, however, has come at a price.

The UIDAI Story

Let me tell the story from the beginning. Governments transfer money to citizens for many reasons—student scholarships, old age pensions, subsidy for LPG cylinders, etc. Such transfers are plagued by the problems of diversion, duplication and falsification, and a large part of the transfers does not reach the genuine beneficiaries. How do we get over these problems?

The answer was to 'identify' each beneficiary by a 'unique' number linked to minimum biometric data. Unique number schemes were not new to the country: the Income Tax Department has a Permanent Account Number (PAN) for each assessee and a credit card bears a unique number for the card holder. In 2009, the UPA government decided to introduce Aadhaar. The Unique Identification Authority of India (UIDAI) was established by an executive order and Mr Nandan Nilekani was roped in to steer the programme and the Authority.

Mr Nilekani brought his tremendous knowledge of technology and proven entrepreneurship to the UIDAI. What might have otherwise turned into another lackadaisical department of the government became a trailblazer on how to design and implement a transformational scheme. After proving the technology and running successful pilots, the UIDAI began enrolling people and issuing Aadhaar in September 2010.

Opposition to the Bill

In order to give the UIDAI a statutory basis, the National Identification Authority of India Bill was introduced in December 2010. It ran into trouble in the Standing Committee on Finance chaired by the formidable Mr Yashwant Sinha, a leading light of the BJP. The Bill languished in Parliament for three years.

Aadhaar faced opposition from social activists who had genuine concerns about exclusion of the un-enrolled and about privacy. In 2013, the Supreme Court, by an interim order, ruled that Aadhaar could not be made mandatory to receive benefits. In 2015, the case was referred to a larger bench to decide the question whether Aadhaar infringed the right to privacy.

Meanwhile, the UIDAI forged ahead with enrolment and the issue of Aadhaar. By March 2014, it had issued unique numbers to 60 crore people (now 99 crore), a record unequalled anywhere in the world. Besides, 24 crore new bank accounts had been opened under the financial inclusion programme. A revolution was under way.

On 1 January 2013, the UPA government launched the Direct

Benefit Transfer (DBT) scheme under which monetary benefits would be transferred directly to the beneficiaries through an Aadhaar-enabled platform. The scheme was rolled out with easy and simple transfers. The big push came when it was mandated that the subsidy for LPG cylinders must be credited directly to Aadhaar-seeded bank accounts.

Right View, Wrong Turn

Fast forward to 2016. The BJP had a change of heart on Aadhaar as on many other matters that it had trashed when it was in the Opposition. The government introduced the Aadhaar (Targeted Delivery of Financial and Other Subsidies, Benefits and Services) Bill, 2016. In the ordinary course, the Bill ought to have gone to the Standing Committee; the report of the Committee discussed; amendments, if any, made; and the Bill passed by both the Houses of Parliament. The ends of the Bill would have been met.

But the government had other plans—and other means. The Bill was introduced in the Lok Sabha as a Money Bill, a reference to the Standing Committee was declined, and the Bill was passed on 11 March 2016. The Rajya Sabha was treated with disdain. Nevertheless, the Rajya Sabha made five amendments. It was late afternoon on 16 March. In the evening, the Lok Sabha, sitting in the extended hours, overrode the amendments and passed the Bill in its original form, and the government claimed a legislative victory!

What Was the Price of the 'Victory'?

1. The Bill was not a Money Bill under Article 110 of the Constitution because it did not 'contain *only* provisions' dealing with the matters enumerated in that Article. The Speaker's decision certifying it as a Money Bill was plainly wrong.
2. The Rajya Sabha was snubbed. It seems that the government depends on the strength of its numbers rather than on the strength of its arguments.
3. The government faces the risk of an adverse verdict. The law could

be struck down on the grounds of violation of fundamental rights and invasion of privacy.

4. The government has incurred the wrath of social activists who feel increasingly alienated. They will carry the debate to the people and doubts and concerns will continue to be aired, casting a shadow on a transformational reform.

The ends were good, the means were bad, and the price was too high.

THEN AND NOW—THE MODEL IS FLAWED

5 June 2016

'Swachh Bharat' or 'Clean India' cannot be a slogan or an event. It has to become a habit, nay, a passion. It involves many factors including:

- Behaviour
- Social structure
- Technology
- Money
- Execution
- Administration

Nirmal Bharat Abhiyan, with the objective of eliminating open defecation by 2017, was apparently designed after taking into account these and other factors. In the early months of its execution, I discovered, in my constituency, that the design was flawed.

Village Social Structure

Sivaganga is a predominantly rural constituency with 627 panchayats, 16 town panchayats and three small municipal towns. The bulk of the population lives in villages. A panchayat has, on average, five or six villages and some hamlets.

In a typical village, habitations or neighbourhoods are organised along caste lines. Each caste group, generally speaking, lives apart. The Dalits, invariably, live in their own quarter. There is acute awareness of one's caste but, for the most part, there is no recurring caste conflict. Village folk have to live and work together for their existence.

Until some years ago, most village dwellings did not have a toilet. People defecated in the open. No one thought open defecation was wrong or unhygienic or a shame. Its most debilitating effect is exposure of children to helminths or intestinal worms (also known as environmental enteropathy) that leads to stunting in children.

As brick houses replaced thatched houses, some houses got toilets. Young men returning from work in cities or towns or with the Army demanded a toilet at home and helped build one. Most members of the family used the toilet. Small children did not, and many women and men preferred open defecation.

How does the government change the behaviour of its citizens in the matter of defecation given the social structure of a village and the limitations of technology, money, execution capability and administration? Nirmal Bharat Abhiyan thought it had the answers, but it did not. Thirty per cent of the toilets built had become dysfunctional. Swachh Bharat thinks it has the answers, but it does not.

Subsidy-Based Models

There are two obvious solutions to the problem of absence of toilets—a private (household) toilet or a community (public) toilet. Let's examine each one of them.

A household toilet cannot be connected to a drainage system, because there is none in the village. Hence, the toilet must be connected to a pit. The pit must be emptied periodically. Usually, the toilet will not have a water tap, and so water must be taken to the toilet by the user. If water is scarce or has to be fetched from a distance, the use of the toilet will diminish. If the whole family, including children, use the toilet it must be cleaned every day, and that will require more water.

The alternative is a community (public) toilet. Before one is built for the village, the following questions must be answered:

1. A public toilet can be built only on government land or acquired land. If the land is in the middle of one habitation, will all caste groups be able to access it every day?
2. If the public toilet is built in or near a Dalit habitation, will the other caste groups use it at all?
3. Because it is a public toilet that will be used round the clock, how will the panchayat ensure adequate supply of water round the clock?
4. The responsibility of keeping the public toilet clean will vest in the panchayat, but who will the panchayat employ for that purpose? The answer is an unspeakable truth in the India of the 21st century, and you know the answer. Few are willing to take up the job of keeping public toilets clean in villages.
5. Will the public toilet be a pay toilet or a free toilet?

In Tamil Nadu, successive governments took up a scheme to build public toilets in villages. I found that most public toilets had been abandoned or had become cattle sheds or dens for drinking and gambling.

Unsurprising Findings

I was therefore not surprised to read the findings of a survey conducted by the National Sample Survey Organisation (NSSO): About 240 lakh household toilets have been built since 2013–14, but 860 lakh toilets remain to be built. In rural India, 57 per cent of the household toilets have no water for use. Forty-four per cent of those toilets had no arrangement for liquid waste disposal and 'it would be safe to presume the residents do not use the toilets'. Of the toilets that had an 'arrangement' for waste disposal, the arrangement in 47 per cent of the cases was draining the waste into a local pond, *nala* or river!

The toilet-building programme requires investment in IEC—information, education and communication—but the money that has been provided is too little (8 per cent of the outlay). The subsidy-based model has been severely criticised. Bangladesh has adopted the Community-led Total Sanitation (CLTS) model that laid emphasis on IEC and has achieved impressive results.

India must rethink its strategy if open defecation must be eliminated by 2019.

Nirmal Bharat Abhiyan failed to achieve its objectives but, at least, it was not converted into a public relations exercise. Swachh Bharat, so far, is an 'event' in the long-running story of event management by the most proficient event managers that the country has seen in a long time.

GOOD SENSE TRIUMPHS, DANGER LURKS

7 August 2016

The first round of the GST Bill is over. There were no losers. The next round is expected in the Winter Session of Parliament, beginning in November 2016. Key issues are still at large, and I wish to begin a debate on them.

Contrary to the impression that the central government may have conveyed to the state finance ministers, the issue of Dispute Resolution has not been settled by the Bill that was passed by the Rajya Sabha recently. Article 131 of the Constitution allows states to file a suit in the Supreme Court for adjudication of disputes between states or between the Centre and one or more states. Besides, there are the well-known provisions such as Articles 32, 226 and 227.

In my view, the provision to establish a dispute settlement mechanism by the GST Council is constitutionally suspect. Be that as it may, assume that the mechanism 'resolves' a dispute between two states. If one of the states is dissatisfied with the verdict, nothing can prevent that state from challenging the decision by way of a suit or a writ petition. To assume that the 'mechanism' will be the final dispute resolution authority reflects a poor understanding of the provisions of the Constitution and the nature of 'judicial power'.

The Standard Rate

A graver issue is the 'standard rate' of GST. The rate of tax is the heart of any tax law. A tax law must specify the rate (like the service tax law) or stipulate ceiling rates that cannot be breached by the executive government (like the excise law). The standard rate (say X) will apply to the vast majority of goods and services. Some goods and services will be zero rated; some goods and services will bear a lower rate (X-); and some demerit goods and services will bear a higher rate (X+).

What should be the standard rate is the question before the country. A committee headed by the government's CEA has presented an excellent report based on sound economic grounds (see box). The Finance Minister did not reject the CEA's report, he only added two caveats:

- that the report did not take into account the cesses imposed after 2013–14;
- that it did not take into account the compensation that the central government had agreed to pay to the state governments for five years.

Report on the Revenue Neutral Rate and Structure of Rates

5.22. Adding up these adjustments yields a single Revenue Neutral Rate (RNR) of 15 per cent. However, we recognise that there may be uncertainty about the adjustments we have made. An alternative scenario is that not all of the adjustments are valid. In this case, the single RNR would be 15.5 per cent.

5.23. Our recommendation for the RNR is, therefore, a range for the RNR of 15–15.5 per cent, with a strong preference for the lower end of that range.

6.5. On structure, in line with growing international practice and with a view to facilitating compliance and administration, India should strive toward a one-rate structure as the medium-term goal.

Meanwhile, we recommend a three-rate structure. In order to ensure that the standard rate is kept close to the RNR, the maximum possible tax base should be taxed at the standard rate. The Committee would recommend the lower rates be kept around 12 per cent (Centre plus states) with standard rates varying between 17 and 18 per cent.

In my view, neither issue affects the conclusions of the report. The cesses may add 1 per cent to the RNR, but the report has suggested a standard rate that is 2.5 to 3 per cent above the RNR. Regarding compensation, the report categorically states, 'In the aggregate, of course, the states should not suffer any loss in revenues because it is intrinsic to the calculation of a revenue neutral rate. That is, if the RNR for the states is set appropriately, states as a whole should have the same revenue as before (para 5.94).'

Socking the People

Moreover, if the government believes that GST will be a more efficient tax that will enhance revenues and reduce tax evasion, it must be prepared to take some risks. All risks cannot be balanced by socking the people with high rates of GST, which is an indirect, and, therefore, regressive tax. The idea of GST has been promoted as pro-growth and pro-people. A high standard rate will be dubbed—and will be seen—as anti-people.

There is, of course, the final question of roll-out of the GST. Two more Bills have to be passed by Parliament. Every state must pass a state GST law. The digital backbone—the GST Network—must be put in place, tested and ready to be operationalised. The GST Council must agree on the rates. Trade and industry must gear up for the new regime. At this stage, no date for the roll-out can be predicted.

Good and Bad Sense

Besides, the roll-out can be smooth only if the government stays on the path of engagement and negotiation. Any attempt to dis-engage with the Opposition or snub the Rajya Sabha will jeopardise the roll-out. The first test of intention will be when the Central-GST and Integrated-GST Bills are introduced in Parliament. Will they be introduced as Money Bills to avoid a meaningful debate and vote in the Rajya Sabha, or as Financial Bills as demanded by all the non-BJP parties?

Good political sense triumphed on 3 August 2016. Bad economic sense or hubris could trip the GST. I keep my fingers crossed.

STATE OF THE ECONOMY

Writing on the state of the economy was the main objective of starting 'Across the Aisle'. It should, therefore, be no surprise that 15 columns were devoted to economic issues. I made sure that I had got my facts and numbers right—no one has pointed out any grave mistake of fact so far. I spent a lot of time collecting the data and also spent a lot of time checking its correctness. My purpose was not to find fault with the government but to identify the fault lines in the economy and suggest measures to fix them. My conclusion is that, in 2016, the economy took a bad hit because of poor diagnosis and wrong prescriptions. I also concluded that on three major tests—jobs, credit growth and private investment—the government had failed.

OIL WINDFALL—GONE WITH THE WIND

14 January 2016

Several statements in the Mid-Year Economic Analysis are intriguing. For example, paragraph 1.4 says, 'It is true that the decline in nominal GDP growth relative to the budget assumption will pose a challenge for meeting the fiscal deficit target of 3.9 per cent of GDP' and quantifies the hit at 0.2 per cent. Nevertheless, paragraph 1.5 asserts, 'As in FY 2015, so too this year, the government's commitment to meet announced fiscal targets is steadfast… If the typical pattern of revenue collection and spending is taken into account, the first half outturn is well in line with meeting the year's target.' That is welcome optimism. It quickly dispelled a momentary doubt. Yet, I was intrigued why the doubt arose in the first place. I was also intrigued by the disarming modesty of the claim that the government will meet the annual target.

Why Not Admit Windfall?

Why is the government shy to admit that it has reaped an oil windfall? In May 2014, Brent crude oil was selling at $109.5 per barrel. In September 2014, it was selling at $97.5 per barrel, and then the crash began. Its impact on the price of the Indian basket of crude oil can be gathered from the following:

- September 2014: $97.0
- October: $85.7
- November: $77.1
- December: $61.1
- January 2015: $46.9

Since January 2015, the price has remained range bound and, in recent weeks, has fallen further. Two days ago, Brent crude price fell below $34 per barrel!

I made an attempt to estimate the 'savings' in the import of crude oil during the period December 2014 to November 2015 compared to the same period of the previous year (December 2013 to November 2014). The comparable average price for the two 12-month periods are $53.6 and $101.3 respectively, a saving of $47.7 per barrel!

In US dollars, the saving is about $40 billion ($93.47–52.74 billion). In Indian rupees, applying the prevailing exchange rates during the respective periods, the saving is estimated at ₹233,000 crore (₹570,000–337,000 crore) during the 12-month period.

Of course, the financial year is April 2015 to March 2016, and hence the estimated saving of ₹233,000 crore may not be accurate. In my view, it would actually be more because crude oil prices have declined further since November 2015.

What Did the Government Gain?

The 'saving' or gain is to the whole economy and will be shared among the government, corporates and households. The next step is to estimate the share of the gain that went to the government. The government has gained in three ways:

1. Additional taxes levied on petroleum and petroleum products after the budget;
2. Lower subsidy bills for fertiliser, LPG and kerosene; and
3. Reduced expenditure on consumption of petroleum products by government departments, especially railways and defence.

I do not wish to burden (or bore) you with the math. I estimate that the government's share will be about 60 per cent of the oil windfall of ₹233,000 crore, that is, about ₹140,000 crore. The more interesting question is, how did, or how will, the government use this gain?

The Controller General of Accounts has reported the revenue and expenditure figures up to November 2015. On the receipts side, net tax revenue, non-tax revenue and recovery of loans are performing better compared to the previous financial year and the five-year moving average. Only capital receipts are lower, presumably because the disinvestment plan is in a shambles. On the expenditure side, as a percentage of the budget estimates up to November, total expenditure is 64.3 per cent, compared to 59.8 per cent last year and the average of 60.4 per cent over the last five years.

Therefore, there is nothing extraordinary about the actual receipts or expenditure of the government so far. No department is expected to spend more than the budgeted amount. No department has been allocated additional funds. No extraordinary promise of funds has been made for any other purpose. There is no indication that the government has pre-paid any loans or has advanced the redemption of bonds to reduce the stock of debt. It seems to be business as budgeted.

Where Did the Gain Go?

So, the question at the end of the year will be, where did the windfall go? I suspect the answers will be:

1. 'We did not achieve the disinvestment target.' That would not be very complimentary to a government that advocates privatisation of public sector enterprises!
2. 'We failed to achieve the tax revenue targets.' If this happens, despite the additional taxes levied post-budget, that would not be very complimentary to the Department of Revenue!
3. 'Lower nominal GDP growth resulted in a higher fiscal deficit.' If the government did not anticipate lower nominal growth despite warnings

(and did not have a Plan B), that would not be very complimentary to a government (and party) that claimed to have all the answers to the challenges faced by the economy!

The gain has been used to fill these gaps. Imagine the benefit that would have accrued to the economy if public investment had got a ₹140,000 crore boost! Imagine the greater welfare that would have accrued if the budget cuts to crucial programmes had been restored!

We got a windfall. And it has gone with the wind.

companies. It is not a zero sum game where the pain of one country will be the gain of another. If China's demand falls, it will import less from India. If commodity prices do not recover, China will continue to dump its products in India and Indian producers will suffer. If the yuan's volatility roils world currency markets, the rupee will also be hit. It is believed that the RBI may have spent $3.6 billion in the first two weeks of January to arrest the depreciation of the rupee. So, in the short run, China's woes may cause us more pain, not less.

Last September, it was reported that the Prime Minister had called a meeting of industry leaders to discuss whether and how India could take advantage of the situation where the Chinese economy appeared to be in trouble. Some advisers are reported to have presented the situation as an 'opportunity' for India. Even now, there are some commentators who believe that India can take 'advantage' of the situation. Such advice is not only misplaced, but could lead to misjudgements and wrong prescriptions for the problems that the country is likely to face.

The Transition

The Prime Minister must indeed initiate a dialogue. The conversation should be about the real issues: the exchange rate and how India should deal with the probability of some depreciation; the travails of Indian producers and how the government can help them in the near term; how to arrest and then reverse the decline in exports; and how to enthuse Indian investors to make investments in the real economy (especially in manufacturing industries) when the reality is that many current projects are either stalled or have been scrapped.

Above all, the Prime Minister must begin a conversation on how to initiate and manage the transition of India's economy that I referred to earlier.

China is not India's sibling, nor is China India's nemesis. It is a country that has recognised the imperative and the difficulties of transiting to a market economy and is struggling to find the right mix of policies. India is in the same situation.

BASKING IN AN ILLUSORY SUNSHINE

3 April 2016

The Revenue Secretary is reported to have sent a missive to the Central Board of Direct Taxes (CBDT) asking the Board to explain why direct taxes collection had fallen short of the revised estimates of 2015–16. That the Revenue Secretary did not wait for the provisional accounts for the year is revealing. I think he gave vent to his frustration.

Why is direct taxes collection an important indicator of economic health?

The Glaring Weaknesses

The budget estimates placed direct taxes collection in 2015–16 at ₹797,995 crore. The revised estimates were scaled down to ₹752,021 crore. The actuals may be less. That means the government was unable to collect more than ₹45,000 crore of the budgeted revenue and the shortfall could rise. That kind of shortfall is an indicator of several weaknesses in the economy:

- Firstly, that the incomes of individuals have fallen and corporate profits have declined steeply;
- Secondly, that individuals and households will put away less money as savings;

- Thirdly, that firms/corporates will have less money to invest in the new financial year;
- Fourthly, wage/salary increases in the organised as well as unorganised sectors will be modest;
- Fifthly, new jobs will be scarce; and
- Sixthly, demand for goods and services by consumers and investors will be muted.

The available data confirm the above weaknesses. Yet, the Prime Minister remains cheerful. Only Mr Modi could have told the Bloomberg India Economic Forum that, thanks to his government's prudent policies, 'the economy is doing well'. Let me examine the main claims made by the Prime Minister on 28 March 2016.

Facile Arguments

1. Claim: To underplay the positive impact of the 70 per cent decline in oil prices, he said, 'Between 2008 and 2009, crude oil prices fell steeply from a peak of $147 per barrel to less than $50. Yet in 2009–10, India's fiscal deficit, current account deficit and inflation rate got substantially worse.'
   Response: Comparison with 2009–10 is manifestly absurd. It was the year when the full impact of the global financial crisis (September 2008) was felt, and global growth had collapsed to 0.028 per cent. It was the mother of all headwinds. Economists named the crisis as the Great Recession. Compare that to the 3.1 per cent growth registered by the world's economy in 2015. Mr Modi's attempt to downplay the oil bonanza is puerile. The government's Economic Survey itself points out that the gain to India has been about 2 per cent of GDP.
2. Claim: To explain the negative export growth for 15 successive months, Mr Modi said, 'We have not been lucky with global trade or growth. Both are low, and have not helped us in terms of export stimulus.'
   Response: To quote the government's Economic Survey, 'The severity of the (export) slowdown—in fact, a decline in export volume—went

beyond adverse external developments'. So, even Mr Modi's own team does not buy his excuse.

3. Claim: Mr Modi cited fiscal consolidation as the main example of 'prudence, sound policy and effective management'.
   Response: The government had, in 2015–16, unwisely stretched the fiscal consolidation timetable by one year. The oil price bonanza resulted in savings worth about 1 per cent of GDP, making fiscal consolidation in 2015–16 much easier. While the fiscal deficit target of 3.5 per cent is praiseworthy, the math is puzzling (see my column 'Budget 2016–17: The Fiscal Math Is Puzzling', dated 13 March 2016).

Facts Prove Claims Wrong

4. Claim: Mr Modi cited indicators such as credit growth and foreign direct investment (FDI).
   Response: The present credit growth of 11.5 per cent is well below the long-term average. Moreover, credit to industry grew at just 5.6 per cent and credit to medium-scale industries actually shrank by 7.15 per cent. In Q3 of 2015–16, FDI was 2.04 per cent of GDP, which is average: it was higher in Q4 of 2007–08 (2.53 per cent), Q1 of 2008–09 (2.79 per cent) and Q2 of 2009–10 (2.43 per cent).
5. Claim: Mr Modi claimed that the government's schemes will double farmers' income by 2022.
   Response: This claim has been rubbished in many articles, including my column on 6 March 2016. It will not happen because farmers' income will not grow at 12 per cent a year.
6. Claim: Mr Modi spoke glowingly about his goal of 'Reform to Transform' and cited several examples.
   Response: Direct transfer of MGNREGA wages, opening of bank accounts under the financial inclusion plan, Food Security Act, etc., were initiatives of the UPA government. Auction of spectrum was first done under the UPA; auction of coal blocks was first done under the NDA. HELP and UDAY are actually HELP II and UDAY II, an attempt to improve upon old policies. The other initiatives are, for

the present, mere announcements.

7. Claim: Mr Modi talked about the initiatives his government has taken to boost employment generation.
   Response: According to Labour Bureau data, new jobs in eight labour-intensive industries fell to 1.55 lakh in the first nine months of 2015, less than half of the number of jobs created in the corresponding period in 2013 and 2014, and less than a quarter of the number in the corresponding period in 2011.

I do not doubt the intentions of the government. My worry is, does the government have a firm grasp of the current economic situation? The dazzle of '7.5 per cent GDP growth' should not blind us to the reality of poor aggregate demand, sputtering investment, stalled exports and near-zero job creation. This is not the time to bask in an illusory sunshine.

A FACTUAL REPORT FROM THE GROUND

10 April 2016

Data is pouring in from diverse sources and one thing is clear: investments are not taking off any time soon. New investment proposals that stood at ₹2,200,000 crore in 2008–09 declined to ₹1,064,000 crore in 2014–15 and further to ₹800,000 crore in 2015–16. Why is this so despite the government's efforts to motivate entrepreneurs to invest? Let me state the main reasons that I have gathered from my talks with businesspersons, bankers and bureaucrats.

1. **Stalled projects:** Every major business group has at least one project that is stalled. The promoter is struggling to pull it out of the woods. While a number of projects have been put back on the rails in the last four years, many more have derailed in the same period. The Centre for Monitoring Indian Economy (CMIE) has put out the following figures of stalled projects at the end of March of the year:

    - 2014: 766
    - 2015: 816
    - 2016: 893

    I wonder what happened to the Project Monitoring Group (PMG) that was set up under the Cabinet Committee on Investment. As long as Mr Anil Swarup (now Secretary, Ministry of Coal) was heading the group, there was visible progress. After he left, the PMG appears to have lost its vigour. Unless stalled projects are back on track, investors will be loath to commit new investments.

Non-Policy Hurdles

2. **Government's inertia:** The data put out by CMIE and HSBC show that 'non-policy' reasons account for 55 per cent of the stalled projects. Land acquisition, environmental clearance, non-environmental approvals and fuel/feedstock supply are listed as 'policy' reasons. The 'non-policy' reasons are unfavourable market conditions, lack of promoter interest, lack of funds and other reasons. I was intrigued to note that lack of promoter interest (16 per cent) and lack of funds (4 per cent) account for 20 per cent of stalled government projects. Even if the government focused on *government* projects alone and resolved the issues affecting them, a lot of investments will turn productive.
3. **The NPA scare:** Non-performing assets (NPAs) are not a new phenomenon. In recent times, the problem of NPAs was acute in 2002 and 2008. Banks had lent the money, so banks must be told to recover the money. There was no need to create a scare of prosecution in every case of NPA. NPAs can be divided into two categories—wilful defaulters and victims of an economic downturn. There has been a downturn in the global economy and the Indian economy. A downturn will claim victims. Most small and medium enterprises that have NPAs are victims and not villains. They need the government and the banks to hold their hand until economic growth picks up in the affected sectors. Bankers will do that if they are left alone and not chastised by all and sundry and, in due course, those loans will be recovered. Wilful defaulters are a separate class. Bankers must be told firmly to use all measures, including enforcing personal guarantees, and they will do their job. The RBI Governor alone seems to have realised the consequences of whipping up mass frenzy over NPAs when he said that a heavy-handed approach 'will kill both entrepreneurship and lending'.

Role of Interest Rate

4. **Interest rate and credit growth:** Whatever one may say, the investor has benchmarked the rate of interest to his rate of return. If his interest cost is high, he feels that his reward will be low, and so he says why risk another investment? That is why it is believed that a lower interest rate will stimulate investment. The RBI has its own constraints in cutting the policy rate; banks have their own problems in lowering lending rates (deposit growth vs credit growth and deposit rates vs lending rates). There is no easy solution. Nevertheless, the government is obliged to find solutions, even if they are only sectoral solutions, and tweak some other instruments (taxes, rebates, subsidies) to compensate the affected sectors. Doing nothing is not an option.

   What is the story of credit flow to industry? Between February 2015 and February 2016, credit growth was 5.36 per cent, which is less than one-half of the average rate of credit growth in the last five years (13.66 per cent). 5.36 per cent growth translates to additional credit of about ₹140,000 crore. Infrastructure (59 per cent) and steel (24 per cent) have cornered 83 per cent of the additional credit. All other sectors got only 17 per cent. Large industries got additional credit of ₹148,000 crore, while small and medium industries suffered a contraction of ₹8,000 crore. The numbers are at odds with the claims of the government about credit support to small and medium industries. These are the problems that cry for attention and redressal.

No Witch Hunt

5. **Suspicion and witch hunt:** Large loans are sanctioned by a committee of the board of directors of a bank. Every large loan that has turned NPA is now viewed with suspicion and, according to bankers, there is a witch hunt. No banker is willing to approve a large loan; no banker is willing to sell the bank's NPAs to an asset management company at a discount. Every banker wants to retire without incident—such

is the atmosphere of suspicion that has been created by thoughtless pronouncements.

The government's intentions may be good, but that is not enough. As the saying goes, the way to hell is paved with good intentions. The government must tackle the problems boldly and take difficult decisions. That alone will promote new investments.

LET'S ADMIT WE ARE CHALLENGED IN ONE EYE

24 April 2016

This government is a bundle of nerves. It sees ghosts where none exists. It sees enemies even among friendly and neutral commentators. And it has men and women who are ready to shoot to kill even without orders (under a political version of AFSPA—Angry Friends Special Powers Act).

What did Dr Raghuram Rajan, Governor, RBI, say that deserved a snub from the Commerce Minister? He said that the estimated growth rate of GDP of about 7.5 per cent makes India the 'one-eyed king in a land of the blind'. The government should be flattered that the Governor had endorsed its estimate of GDP growth.

The Dichotomy

Going by GDP growth alone, India is at the top among large economies, notwithstanding the dichotomy between the GDP growth rate and other economic indicators. Compare 2015–16 with two years that had almost similar growth rates (see table) and the dichotomy is visible.

Be that as it may, India could well be the fastest growing large economy in 2016 (or 2016–17). Next in line are China at 6.5 per cent (on a base that is five times bigger) and the Philippines at 6.3 per cent. Of the BRICS countries, Brazil (-3.6) and Russia (-1.5) are expected to register negative growth and South Africa a small, positive growth of 0.7 per cent. Crude oil, India's benefactor, has been the spoiler in the cases of Brazil and Russia.

	1999–2000	*2004–05*	*2015–16*
GDP growth	7.59	6.97	7.3 (new series)
Growth in Gross Fixed Capital Formation (GFCF)	7.93	23.98	5.3
Exports	10.64	30.7	-15.82
Imports	3.26	41.69	-4.16
Growth in Index of Industrial Production	6.62	11.00	2.61 (from February 2015 to February 2016)
Growth in non-food credit	16.55	31.62	11.48 (from February 2015 to February 2016)
Growth in bank deposits	13.91	13.01	10.27 (from February 2015 to February 2016)
Inflation (March year–on–year)	3.4	2.4	4.83

(figures in per cent)

The Other Eye

One eye may seem bright. That is the eye of growth, foreign investment and aspiration. But there is another eye. That is the eye of fiscal stability, employment, education, healthcare, inflation, poverty ratio and other parameters that are equally important indicators of a healthy and growing economy. In that eye, India has poor vision.

Take, for example, the budget balance. Of the 42 significant countries tracked by *The Economist* magazine, India's fiscal deficit (-3.9 per cent) was larger than the fiscal deficit (or surplus) of 33 countries. We still have a long way to go on the road to fiscal stability.

India's inflation, although declining since November 2013, is still comparatively high. At 5.2 per cent, it is higher than the inflation of every other country tracked by *The Economist*, except South Africa (6.2 per cent), Brazil and Turkey (8.3 per cent), Russia (8.4 per cent) and

Egypt (8.8 per cent).

Unemployment is a key indicator. Official data for India released in January 2015 puts it at 4.9 per cent, a gross underestimate because of factors such as underemployment, low workforce participation, gender disparity and informalisation.

The benchmark interest rate (on 10-year government bonds) for India is 7.44 per cent, much above the comparable rates of most advanced and emerging economies. Countries with higher interest rates are the faltering economies—Greece, Russia, Turkey, Pakistan, Brazil, Colombia, Venezuela and South Africa. High interest rates erode competitiveness.

I shall write a separate column on how far behind our peers India is on human development indices.

Pragmatic Governor

Dr Rajan was, therefore, spot on when he underplayed GDP growth. He was not disparaging India's growth rate; he was gently reminding the government that much more remains to be done. I may add my voice and remind the government that in five out of the 10 years of the UPA government, the growth rate exceeded 8.5 per cent. The average for the 10 years was 7.54 per cent (old series). Impressive as 7.5 per cent (new series) may be, there is unfinished work.

Dr Rajan was not obliged to explain what he had meant, but he did explain a few days later and reminded his critics that a central banker has 'to be pragmatic and cannot get euphoric'. The *raj dharma* of the Commerce Minister is to devote her whole time and energy to address the problems of India's trade sector, which was marked by a terrible export performance in 2015–16 that was 16 per cent lower than the performance in 2014–15. That black spot alone has consequences, such as worsening the current account deficit, putting millions of jobs in jeopardy, and driving thousands of small and medium enterprises into the NPA column and possible closure.

While Dr Rajan's choice of words is being needlessly debated, I think the Commerce Minister's choice of silence as a response to criticism is inexcusable.

WANTED—A BHARATANATYAM DANCER, PLEASE

8 May 2016

In a caustic comment on an economist, Dr Jagdish Bhagwati once said, 'If he is an economist, I'm a Bharatanatyam dancer!' Dr Arvind Panagariya is an honourable man. He has a job to do, but has a useless tool—the NITI Aayog (National Institution for Transforming India)—in his hands. The NITI Aayog is neither an all-powerful arbiter of policy differences and fund allocation, nor is it a fountainhead of new ideas and systemic changes. The NITI Aayog is in no man's land and is all but forgotten.

The disappointment of Dr Panagariya can be seen in his recent article in a newspaper. However, he has carefully qualified his views by noting that 'views are personal and may not be attributed to either the Government of India or NITI Aayog'.

Astonishing Statements

In venting his frustration, Dr Panagariya has made some astonishing statements. Here are a few excerpts:

- 'In May 2004, (the NDA) handed to the UPA an economy that had grown 8.1 per cent during the preceding full year;

- Under UPA I ... growth averaged 8.4 per cent. There is no satisfactory answer to the question, "What UPA I did to make it happen?"... You will find references to few reforms to which this performance can be attributed;
- The economic reform process that PM Rao had launched and PM Vajpayee had accelerated experienced a sudden stop under UPA;
- The result was that an economy which had seemed unstoppable and had grown at the average rate of 8.1 per cent during the first three years of UPA II rule, descended into what appeared to be a crisis.'

After making these damaging—and egregiously wrong—statements, Dr Panagariya was forced to conclude that 'much change in policy has taken place since May 2014 and the miracle-level annual growth of 8.3 per cent that India saw from 2003–04 to 2011–12 is poised to return'.

The NDA and UPA Records

When the UPA assumed office in May 2004, the economy was *not* growing at the rate of 8.1 per cent. No one in his right mind will pick one year to describe the trend growth rate. The growth rates of the NDA years were:

- 1999–00: 7.6 per cent
- 2000–01: 4.3 per cent
- 2001–02: 5.5 per cent
- 2002–03: 4.0 per cent
- 2003–04: 8.1 per cent

The compounded average for the five years was 5.9 per cent. The 'bounce' in 2003–04 was because of the low base of the previous year and after three years of sub-par performance.

Every commentator has acknowledged that the best years of the Indian economy ('boom years', according to the current CEA) were 2004–09, that is the period of UPA I. The economy was riding a high wave (over 9 per cent) when, in September 2008, the world economy was struck by a major financial crisis. Despite the crisis that devoured many economies, India registered a growth rate of 6.7 per cent in 2008–09, and the compounded average for the five years was an unprecedented 8.4 per cent. I wonder if Dr Panagariya recalls that crisis, because he makes no mention of it in his article.

Dr Panagariya says that he could find few reforms to which the performance of UPA I could be attributed. In a column titled 'What Is Economic Reform, What Is Not' (*The Indian Express*, 29 November 2015), I had listed 11 true reform measures that had transformed the nature of India's economy. One of them was initiated when Mr Vajpayee was Prime Minister and three under the UPA. Add to the list other changes and measures that have wider socio-economic benefits such as MGNREGA, RTI and the National (New) Pension System. Also, add the reservation of 27 per cent for the Other Backward Class (OBCs) and the substantial increases, year after year, in the allocations for health and education. The UPA's record is substantial.

In every respect, the best year was 2007–08. Post the 2008 crisis, India was faced with a hard choice. Should we stick to the path of fiscal consolidation and allow sound fundamentals to propel growth? Or should we follow the textbook and stimulate the flagging economy to maintain high growth? The government decided to implement three stimulus packages in succession. The result was that high growth was ensured for three years, but the fiscal deficit, current account deficit and Consumer Price Index (CPI) inflation went completely out of line.

The last two years of UPA II (2012–13 and 2013–14) were devoted to putting the economy back on track. We succeeded in large measure: the fiscal deficit was brought down from 5.73 per cent in 2011–12 to 4.43 per cent in 2013–14 and the current account deficit from $78 billion to $32 billion in the same period. Inflation began to decline from November 2013. However, growth was tepid at 4.47 per cent and 4.74 per cent (under the old series).

The rates have since been revised by the NDA government to 5.1 per cent and 6.9 per cent (new series).

Growth under a Shadow

Does Dr Panagariya not believe the revised growth rate of 6.9 per cent? If he has no faith in his government's numbers, how does he claim that growth has steadily climbed to 7.2 per cent in 2014–15 and 7.6 per cent in 2015–16?

Finally, what is the 'much change in policy' that Dr Panagariya has alluded to? He does not name one major reform by the current government that will accelerate the rate of growth. The economy is growing under a shadow of uncertainty: without creating jobs; with a collapse of the export sector; with poor credit growth; with low household savings; and with a private sector that is shy of making new investments.

I apologise to Dr Panagariya, but I must say that a Bharatanatyam dancer would have brought greater clarity to the subject of the state of the economy.

I WISH THE PRIME MINISTER HAD SAID

29 May 2016

My fellow citizens, brothers and sisters,

I greet you on this day, 26 May 2016, when my government completes two years in office. The usual practice is to make a self-congratulatory speech and repeat old promises or make new promises. I have decided to break from this tradition and present an honest and objective assessment of the state of the nation.

Uppermost on your minds is the economy. Today, a leading business newspaper began its editorial with the words 'As the Narendra Modi government completes two years in office; the economic recovery that began in the last quarter of 2013 continues to gather momentum...'

Inherited Stable Economy

That is correct. The recovery had begun in 2013 under the UPA government. The economy had been stabilised after the volatile years of 2008–2012: inflation had begun its steady decline from 11.5 per cent in November 2013 to 6.7 per cent in June 2014, the fiscal deficit had been contained at 4.4 per cent at the end of 2013–14, the current account deficit had been compressed to 1.7 per cent, and the foreign exchange reserves stood at a healthy $314 billion. Yet, everyone agreed that there were headwinds and the new government faced important challenges.

Two years after, I am glad to report that we have some achievements to our credit. Helped by unprecedented low oil and commodity prices, we were able to bring down the CPI inflation from 6.7 per cent in June 2014 to 5.4 per cent in April 2016. After a half step in 2015–16, which was a mistake, we decided in February 2016 to return to the path of fiscal consolidation, and I assure you that we will reach the target of 3 per cent in 2017–18.

I believe the Central Statistics Office (CSO) numbers which said that the UPA government had bequeathed an economy that had grown at 6.9 per cent in 2013–14. The growth rates were 7.2 per cent in 2014–15 and 7.6 per cent (estimated) in 2015–16. Even allowing for some overstatement, the new 'normal' for India's GDP appears to be about 7 per cent. That, however, is not sufficient.

The keys to high growth are fiscal stability, enabling policies and increased investment. And it is high growth that will bring jobs. Among parents and young people, the main concern is jobs. A report, based on a survey, published today by a government-friendly newspaper, has listed the expectations of the people. They are creation of jobs; tackling drought and farmers' woes; and bringing down inflation. Development and economic growth is the demand of the people (56 per cent). By way of contrast, only 10 per cent demand promotion of Hindutva. Even if some in my party or government take a different view, I am determined to heed the voice of the people.

Failed in Job Creation

To be absolutely candid, we failed to create jobs. We also failed to anticipate and tackle rural distress, especially among farmers and farm labourers. The agriculture sector shrank by -0.2 per cent and grew by 1.1 per cent in the last two years. I am mindful of Dr Ashok Gulati's admonition today that 'the government needs to move fast and deploy bold steps on the agri-front if it wants the farming community to benefit and poverty eliminated'.

Our moderately successful stories are in building roads, power generation and production of fertilisers. We have also achieved significant success in areas where we have taken forward the programmes of the previous government. I know that my party, including me, had rubbished MGNREGA and questioned the legality and utility of Aadhaar. I have no hesitation in admitting that we were wrong. While change is necessary, there is merit in continuing with the well-designed schemes and programmes of the previous government.

Similarly, my government has greatly benefited by the Nirmal Bharat Abhiyan and the National Skill Development Mission launched by the previous government. We have scaled up the two programmes, which are now being implemented as Swachh Bharat and Skill India.

Many Mountains to Climb

However, we have many more mountains to climb. Several growth indicators are worrying. Among them are annual sales of all firms (-5.77 per cent), annual sales of manufacturing firms (-11.15 per cent), credit (9.77 per cent), merchandise exports (-15.55 per cent) and the index of industrial production (2.4 per cent). What this means is that while the economy is capable of maintaining its pace, its overall health is not robust. A new 'normal' growth rate of 7 per cent will not create jobs, especially for the millions of young people who have no more than 8 or 10 years of school education and no special skills. Our demographic dividend may turn out to be a demographic millstone if we cannot create useful jobs for the approximately one crore people who enter the job market every year.

I have, therefore, directed the ministries concerned to immediately propose suitable measures to implement the following prescriptions:

- Find finances for infrastructure projects, including new financing structures for long-term funds and pooling of investments.
- Evolve a policy for manufacturing for export.
- Rebuild all cities with a new model of governance to make them liveable cities.
- Prepare a timetable to implement the recommendations of the Financial Sector Legislative Reforms Commission.

Above all, I intend to enlist the support of the Opposition parties through discussion and accommodation of their views.

I have dwelt at length on the economy. There are other equally weighty issues. Let me now address those issues….

GROSS DOMESTIC PRODUCT OR PUZZLE?

12 June 2016

It was good that Dr Raghuram Rajan, Governor, RBI, has cleared some of the mist—and myth—surrounding the GDP numbers. He gave two simple examples:

- 'Exports minus imports' is a contributory factor to GDP. Exports declined in 2015–16, but imports declined even more. So, 'exports minus imports' in 2015–16 was greater than 'exports minus imports' in 2014–15. That means growth, contributing to the GDP number (in current prices)!
- 'Sales minus input costs' is another contributory factor to GDP. Sales of all manufacturing firms declined by 9.02 per cent in 2015–16 over the previous year, but input costs declined more sharply (18.42 per cent), thanks to the steep fall in oil and commodity prices. Consequently, 'sales minus input costs' was greater in 2015–16 than in 2014–15. Result is growth!

Output Declines, Growth Rises!

In both cases, there was no increase in output. Exporters exported less, factories produced less, firms had lower turnovers, there was little or no additional employment, and yet the sectoral 'growth' figures of the export sector and the manufacturing sector were positive, leading to the illusion that export and manufacturing sectors had 'grown' at a brisk pace. (Here, I assume that productivity remained constant.) Since the two sectors contributed significantly to the overall GDP number, the GDP number got a boost.

The steep decline in oil and commodity prices is a new phenomenon, and I think the CSO is not equipped to construct credible growth numbers in such a situation. The disconnect between the numbers and the reality on the ground is very evident. No amount of rationalisation can change the reality that is felt every day by the citizens—CPI inflation upwards of 5 per cent, no new visible investment and no additional jobs on offer. The average person is, therefore, stunned when he is told that the GDP had grown at 7.6 per cent.

We get a more realistic picture of the economy if we look at the output numbers. Of the eight core industries, coal, refinery products, fertilisers, cement and electricity produced more in 2015–16, while crude oil, natural gas and steel produced less than in the previous year. The growth in the Index of Industrial Production of the eight core industries in 2015–16 was only 2.67 per cent. Nevertheless, the CSO reported high growth in the three sectors (that encompass the eight industries), namely, mining and quarrying (7.44 per cent), manufacturing (9.29 per cent) and electricity and gas (6.57 per cent)!

Deficiencies in Methodology

Ever since the CSO moved to the new method of calculation, there has been growing scepticism. Analysts have pointed to several aspects of the new methodology that are suspect. One of the main deficiencies was the choice of deflators. Gross value additions (GVA) are measured in current prices, but in order to make them comparable with measurements based on prices in the base year (2011–12), one must 'deflate' them with an appropriate deflator. In the cases of 'trade, hotels, transport, communication etc.' and 'financial, real estate and professional services', the GVA at current prices was 6.6 per cent and 7.4 per cent, respectively. The CSO applied *negative* deflators and reported a growth rate of 9 per cent and 10.3 per cent respectively. When the 12-month average of CPI inflation in 2015–16 was 4.9 per cent, it is difficult to believe that inflation in these two sectors was negative! There has been no convincing explanation why negative deflators were chosen for these two service sectors.

The second deficiency was the use of the MCA21 database. It has been admitted that the database requires to be stabilised. We also know, anecdotally, that small and medium firms find it difficult to report the data about their firms periodically in the new format. Besides, the MCA21 database has been shared only with the CSO, and no one has been able to verify the correctness of the data.

The GDP growth number is an approximation of the underlying economic activity. Many economic decisions of the government and private investors are based on that number. My analysis leads to the conclusion that the GDP number is not 'as accurate as possible' and certainly does not inspire confidence. Some corrections are, therefore, in order.

Corrections Needed

The first correction must be to identify industries and sectors where quantitative output had declined in 2015–16 over 2014–15 (productivity assumed as constant) and assume that growth in such industry/sector was zero. Examples would be exports, crude oil, natural gas and steel.

The second correction would be to revisit the deflators that were used. There is a huge divergence between Wholesale Price Index (WPI) inflation and CPI inflation. It makes no sense to use negative deflators for sectors (especially services) where oil and commodity prices have no role to play and where consumer prices have, in fact, increased.

The third correction is to reconstruct the GDP numbers using the old, conventional data and release them alongside the numbers using the MCA21 database until the MCA21 database is believed to have been stabilised.

Finally, there is no harm in publishing, at least for a few years, GDP numbers using the old method and the new method. The CSO should complete the following table and restore credibility to the whole exercise.

Year	*Old Method*	*New Method*
2012–13	4.47	5.62*
2013–14	4.74	6.64*
2014–15	?	7.2
2015–16	?	7.6

**as revised*

My guess is that the number for each of the question mark-years would be between 5 and 5.5 per cent.

ECONOMIC REFORMS—ACT I, SCENE I

26 June 2016

Twenty-five years ago, the mood of the people of India was one of fear and despair. The nation was in the middle of an election. Two hundred and twenty-one constituencies had voted; the remaining had yet to vote. Rajiv Gandhi was killed in a bomb blast on 21 May 1991, and elections in the remaining constituencies were postponed. When those elections took place in June, the mood of the people swung in favour of the Congress. In the end, the Congress got 226 seats, but was without a majority or a leader.

Meanwhile, the economy was sputtering. By end-March 1991, foreign exchange reserves had plunged to an all-time low of $5.8 billion and were falling by the day. Fear of the unknown was written everywhere.

Unexpected Choices

The Congress seized the opportunity as only a responsible and experienced political party could. In a remarkable display of unity and maturity, the Congress held an election to choose the leader, P.V. Narasimha Rao, who easily beat Mr Sharad Pawar, and a new government was sworn in on 21 June 1991.

It was a typical Congress government, a mix of the old and the young, and balancing caste and region. It was different only because the

Prime Minister was a quiet, self-effacing person, unglamorous and largely 'unknown' to the people of India. Eyebrows were raised on the choice of the Finance Minister—Dr Manmohan Singh, an economist and bureaucrat, who had held various key offices in government, without making waves.

The first week of the new government was unusually quiet. The Congress was happy that it had returned to power, but there were no celebrations. I was amused by Narasimha Rao's question to the Cabinet Secretary at the first meeting of the Council of Ministers: 'Have you arranged *ghoda/gaadi* for everyone?' Nothing remarkable was expected of the government, and certainly no one expected that a revolution would be ignited in a few days.

My sense is that external events unfolded so rapidly and relentlessly that the government was forced to act. It was a remarkable stroke of luck that three able men were in key positions: Dr Singh as Finance Minister, the extraordinarily intelligent Mr S. Venkitaramanan as Governor, RBI, and the extraordinarily capable Dr C. Rangarajan as Deputy Governor.

Courageous, but No Celebration

As foreign exchange reserves plummeted, the government had no choice but to 'correct' the official exchange rate—a euphemism for devaluation. In a clever move, the RBI decided to do it in two steps, the first on 1 July 1991 (to test the waters) and the second on 3 July. The public reaction to the first 'correction' was muted, but the 'establishment' developed cold feet. Narasimha Rao wanted the second step scrapped, but the wily Dr Rangarajan made himself 'unavailable' to telephone calls from Delhi (there were no mobile phones), most probably with the concurrence of Dr Manmohan Singh! Thus began, with a bang, what is universally acknowledged as a new era in the economic history of India.

The 25 years that have rolled by have changed the face of India and the fortunes of millions of people who have been lifted out of poverty. I was lucky to have had a part in the various Acts of the drama that continues to play even today—the script was more or less the same, only the key actors changed from time to time.

The other difference—actually the BIG difference—is that while dramatic changes were being made to the economic policy, the government maintained a low profile and avoided any drama or hype. There were no choreographed 'events'; even full-page advertisements were avoided. The first major exposition of the new policies was on 4 July, at a seminar in Delhi. In September, Dr Manmohan Singh and I travelled to Singapore to address an India-specific conference that attracted investors and bankers from around the world.

Looking back, the milestones that we crossed in the first year (1991–92) were truly amazing:

- 1 July 1991: First step devaluation
- 3 July: Second step devaluation
- 4 July: Initial changes in Trade Policy
- 4–18 July: Pledged gold transferred to the Bank of England
- 24 July; 11 a.m.—New Industrial Policy Resolution; 5 p.m.—Budget for 1991–92
- 13 August: Major changes in Trade Policy
- 28 February 1992: Budget for 1992–93
- 31 March: New Import–Export Policy

The Philosophical Context

It is wrong to think that economic reforms consist of announcements or a few deft strokes of the pen making changes in some policy or other. Changes have to be in the context of an overarching economic and social philosophy. It was never stated explicitly, but I can say with confidence that the key players in 1991, beginning with Narasimha Rao, believed in the following:

- Getting government out of gratuitous interventions in the markets;
- Getting government into addressing the notable market failures through regulation (capital market, banking, anti-competition, etc.);
- Building capacity in government to do the things it must do (taxation, delivery of public goods and services, etc.);

- Expanding freedoms for the people (economic, social, religious, etc.).

My assessment of what has been achieved in the 25 years is that while we have done reasonably well on the first two points, we have failed on point three and we are struggling to find our way—maybe lost our way—on point four. That is a sobering thought on the 25th anniversary.

ECONOMIC REFORMS—THE NEXT FRONTIERS

10 July 2016

The past week marked the 25th anniversary of economic reforms and the liberalisation of the Indian economy. The government ignored the occasion and the reason was not far to seek: the reforms were ushered in by a Congress government under P.V. Narasimha Rao and the BJP had, at that time, stoutly opposed them. (The Swadeshi Jagaran Manch survives to this day.) Imagine if Mr Vajpayee had been Prime Minister in 1991 (rather than in 1998)—the government would have gone to town with its own brand of celebrations!

The Congress party also did not commemorate the occasion in a significant manner. Dr Manmohan Singh, in his modest way, recalled the events of 1991, and gave credit to all those who deserved credit—although his contribution was the mightiest.

Don't Celebrate, Reflect

I am not unhappy that we have not rejoiced on the achievements of the last 25 years. Celebrations or not, no one can take away the fact that millions of people were lifted out of poverty—of which 140 million were lifted during the period 2004–14. No one can take away the fact that India, today, is a more open and more competitive economy and that we have a place at the high tables of the International Monetary Fund (IMF), World

Bank, Asian Development Bank (ADB), G-20, World Trade Organization (WTO), Bank for International Settlements (BIS), etc.

I am, however, unhappy that we are not reflecting on the lessons learned in the last 25 years and on the new frontiers to be conquered in the next 25 years. Why are the next 25 years the most critical in the history of India?

For centuries—stretching back to perhaps 3,000 years—India has been a poor country or, more accurately, a country of poor people. I believe that, for the first time, we are lifting people out of poverty instead of pushing people into poverty. I also believe that in the next 25 years we have a good chance of wiping out poverty completely—in the case of at least 100 million people, it is abject poverty. If I had said this 25 years ago, I would have been laughed out of court by most people who believed that poverty is the fate of Indians. In the last 25 years, we have broken that fatalistic mindset.

India has a tryst with destiny, but we will fail if a significant proportion of the people is left out of the development process. The main reasons are two: poor education and poor healthcare.

School System in a Shambles

Our school education system is in a shambles. Most children have no option but to go to a government/municipal school. The quality of education provided to them is abysmal. There is often no proper classroom; no library or laboratory; and no educational aids. Teachers are absent (sometimes in pre-arranged turns); many teachers fail a knowledge or skills test. A fifth-grade student cannot do a third-grade math sum. A so-called 'topper' pronounces 'political science' as 'prodigal science' and describes it as a subject dealing with cooking. It is a miracle that some students pass out of such schools with credit and go on to achieve distinction in college or university.

The Sarva Shiksha Abhiyan and the Right to Education Act were intended to remedy the situation. While there has been a quantitative expansion of educational facilities (reflected in higher enrolment), there has been practically no improvement in the quality of education imparted in public schools.

Crumbling Healthcare

Healthcare is no better. There has been a quantitative expansion of the Primary Health Centre (PHC) scheme, but it is still bedevilled by the absence of doctors, nurses, medicines and equipment. Government hospitals at all levels are overburdened. Beds are scarce, medicines have to be purchased by the patient, basic tests or procedures are not done free of cost, and waiting lists for appointments or surgeries are too long. Block- and taluk-level hospitals have become mere referral hospitals. The Universal Health Scheme is a non-starter.

The only way in which we can accelerate and sustain the pace of development is to ensure that every able-bodied adult can work and contribute to economic development. A poorly educated workforce or an unhealthy workforce cannot acquire a competitive edge or improve productivity.

If the Indian economy grows at 6 per cent or 7 per cent or 8 per cent, it will continue to attract FDI. Money will flow into India. Infrastructure will be built. Factories will come up. Doing business will become easier in course of time. Regulations will be more helpful to growth. But a poorly educated and unhealthy workforce will be a severe drag on the economy.

The next frontiers to be conquered are 'school education' and 'primary and secondary healthcare'. The goal must be to make both universal and completely free. The best ministers and the best civil servants must be tasked with managing education and healthcare. The fact that state governments and the central government share authority on these two subjects need not be an obstacle. The economic and electoral dividends of improving education and healthcare will motivate the Centre and the states to work together and there will be room for experimentation.

Don't regret if you were too young to have participated in the reforms process of the last 25 years; the next 25 years will be more challenging and eventful.

AWAITING SPACE FOR POLICY ACTION

14 August 2016

Dr Raghuram Rajan will lay down the office of Governor, RBI, on 4 September 2016. It is a pity that the government has eased him out at the end of three years when he would have willingly served until September 2018 and, if nudged, until the government's term ended in May 2019.

Anyway, let us put those events behind us. Maybe the government will surprise everybody by making an inspired choice. I certainly look forward to the announcement which is already overdue. What awaits the new Governor? To his successor, and to the Prime Minister and the government, Dr Rajan has left valuable messages.

Plain English

Central Bank Governors do not speak in plain English (or French or German or Chinese)! They speak in an elliptical language leaving the listeners to make their own interpretations. Mr Alan Greenspan, a former Chairman of the US Fed, once famously told the US Congress, 'Gentlemen, since I've become a central banker, I've learned to mumble with great incoherence. If I seem unduly clear to you, you must have misunderstood what I said.' Dr Rajan's last policy statement, made on 9 August 2016, was in plain English and could have left no one in doubt. The RBI is not yet prepared to cut the policy rate. Let me cull out a few important statements from the policy:

- 'Since the statement of June 2016, several developments have clouded the outlook for the global economy. Across advanced economies, growth in Q2 of 2016 has been slower than anticipated, and outlook is still mixed.'
- 'Among emerging market economies, activity remains varied.'
- 'World trade remains sluggish in the first half of 2016. Most financial markets did not anticipate the Brexit vote and equities plunged worldwide, currency volatility increased and investors herded into safe havens.'

Configuration of Risks

- '(In India) the prolonged sluggishness in the capital goods sector is indicative of weak investment demand… Business confidence is also looking up in recent months, though the Reserve Bank's survey for March 2016 suggests that capacity utilisation, seasonally adjusted, is still weak.'
- 'Retail inflation measured by the headline CPI rose to a 22-month high in June, with a sharp pick-up in momentum overwhelming favourable base effects.'
- 'In the external sector, merchandise export growth moved into positive territory in June after 18 months… On the other hand, imports continued to decline, albeit at a slower pace than in recent months.'
- 'On balance, inflation projections, as given in the June bi-monthly statement, that is, of a central trajectory towards 5 per cent by March 2017 with risks tilted to the upside, are retained.' [The chart gives a range of 4.8 to 6.4 per cent.]
- 'In view of this configuration of risks, it is appropriate for the Reserve Bank to keep the policy repo rate unchanged at this juncture, while awaiting space for policy action.'

There are, of course, other statements that highlight the positive indicators such as positive outlook for value-added in agriculture, pick-up in industrial orders, expansion in the services sector, moderate rise in rural wages, likely easing in food inflation, positive net portfolio inflows, and ample liquidity. Nevertheless, the message to the government is clear: The RBI is awaiting action of the government that will create space for policy action by the RBI.

Where Are the Triggers?

We come back, again and again, to the absence of triggers to boost the economy. In the absence of triggers, there is no demand for credit from the manufacturing sector (as admitted by many public sector bank chiefs); there is little greenfield industrial investment; there is no evidence of job creation; and there is no 'feel' among the people that the economy is growing at 7.6 per cent.

Who has the hand on the wheel? For example, the Minister of Coal announced that availability of coal is abundant. True, but why are coal stocks piling up leading to cutback in coal production? The Minister of Power claimed that there is no shortage of production of electricity. True, but at what price is electricity available, why is there 'load shedding' by distributors and 'back down' by power plants and, when per capita consumption is low, why is there no demand for electricity?

There are three indicators that must be tracked every month by the government. Firstly, how many stalled projects have moved forward towards commercial operation date (COD); secondly, what is the capacity utilisation at present in each industry; and, thirdly, how many new factories commenced production and how many new jobs were created?

The Governor was right when he said that he is awaiting space for policy action. What he left unsaid is also pretty clear: it is only when action is taken by the government that the RBI will be persuaded to cut the policy rate. Given this situation, I think the government is obliged to tell the nation what it intends to do on sluggish demand, stalled projects, slow credit growth, high food inflation, depressed manufacturing sector and low job creation, so that the RBI, under the next Governor, and the new MPC, will be persuaded to cut the policy rate. Otherwise, the blame game will continue without yielding any result.

The messenger has left a clear message and has packed his bags. Thankfully, the potshots at the Governor have, by and large, stopped. In 20 days from today, the messenger would have left and only the message will remain.

HOW FREE IS FREEDOM IN INDIA?

2 October 2016

Twenty-five years after the Congress government under P.V. Narasimha Rao ushered in 'liberalisation' of the economy, India has still not come to terms with the idea of economic freedom. This is disappointing for a country that was at the forefront of the struggle for political freedom for all countries.

We understand political democracy, but we do not understand economic democracy. I confess that I was a convert to the idea of an open, liberal and competitive economy after flirting with socialism in my formative years.

Freedom Is Indivisible

Political freedom and economic freedom go together. I urge you to take a look at Article 19 of the Constitution (as originally incorporated) that, along with Articles 14 and 21, constitutes the core of the fundamental rights enshrined in the Constitution that we 'gave unto ourselves'. The founding fathers were wise and placed political and economic rights on a par. Freedom of speech and expression [clause (a)] was on a par with freedom to carry on a business, trade or profession [clause (g)]. Freedom to form an association [clause (c)] was on a par with freedom to hold property [clause (f)]. The founding fathers understood how one set of freedoms reinforced the other and how each set would be meaningless without the other.

A little-known set of Articles of the Constitution is a group consisting of Articles 301 to 305. If it had been interpreted correctly, Article 301 would have ushered in the idea of 'One Nation, One Economy'. The Article declared that 'Trade, commerce and intercourse throughout the territory of India shall be free'. That bold idea was smothered by interpretation and scuttled in implementation. State governments and rent-seekers were happy—until they were called out in the few cases that reached the higher courts.

Governments restrict economic freedom in many ways. Once upon a time, the regime was so oppressive that it gave rise to the infamous description of India's governance model as the 'licence-permit-quota raj'. Some restrictions are justified as legitimate requirements, such as registering a business or getting environmental clearance. They are legitimate, but the legitimacy is mostly eroded by the inordinate amount of time it takes to get that piece of paper.

How Does India Fare?

Every year, the World Bank publishes a study called the Ease of Doing Business report. It ranks countries on 10 parameters such as Starting a Business, Getting Electricity, Registering Property, Getting Credit, Paying Taxes and Enforcing Contracts. Between 2015 and 2016, India's rank remained the same or worsened on 7 of the 10 parameters. It improved only on three parameters, but even on these three counts, there is nothing to crow about. On Starting a Business, India's rank improved from 164 to 155, on Dealing with Construction Permits from 184 to 183, and Electricity from 99 to 70. On Getting Credit, the rank had worsened from 36 to 42, on Paying Taxes, it is 157 and on Enforcing Contracts, it is a lowly 178. Overall, India's rank in 2016 is 130 out of 189 countries. Compared with emerging market economies, India ranks 22 out of 23 economies, with only Egypt below us.

Since the 1960s, we have approached the issue of 'freedom vs control' from the wrong end. We started with 'control' and then looked at relaxations bit by bit. The correct approach is the exact opposite. We must start with 'freedom' and then look at the minimum regulations necessary to ensure a level-playing field and compliance with the laws. The first time that I attempted the latter approach was in 1991–92, when we made a bonfire of the dreaded Red Book (that controlled exports and imports) and wrote, in plain English, a 100-page Import–Export Policy. I tried that approach again with the Direct Taxes Code: there are three versions of the Code gathering dust, but the government has declared, unfortunately, that it is not inclined to replace the 55-year-old Income Tax Act.

The other way in which the State interferes with economic freedom is in the purported exercise of its power to punish wrongdoers. I think it is a waste of the State's time, energy and resources if it goes about looking for 'wrongs' and 'wrongdoers' in every activity. When administrative or business decisions are taken, mistakes will be committed, but every mistake is not a 'wrong' that must be investigated and punished. In matters concerning the economy, the State must punish only egregious wrongdoing that has large externalities and baneful consequences.

We Are Mostly Unfree

The Heritage Foundation and *The Wall Street Journal* publish an annual Index of Economic Freedom based on ten factors of 'economic freedom'. India's rank is 123 out of 178 countries, placing us in the 'mostly unfree' category. The World Economic Forum's Global Competitiveness Index measures the 'competitiveness' of an economy, and India's rank, released a few days ago, is 39 out of 138 economies; but on some key parameters such as health and primary education, higher education, labour market efficiency and technological readiness, India is at 81 or lower. These are wake-up calls. Lack of economic freedom, low competitiveness and obstacles to doing business hurt investment, growth, job creation, consumers and, above all, poor people and poor regions.

Despite the reforms since 1991, which is a remarkable story, the State-to-firm interface remains a problem. What needs to be done and what can be done deserve a separate column and I hope to be able to write one soon.

BAD IDEAS WILL DRIVE OUT THE GOOD

9 October 2016

We have a new Governor of the RBI, we have an MPC, and we have their first statement on monetary policy. It is tempting to read the tea leaves!

The MPC's statement, with unanimous support, is significant not only for the cut in the policy repo rate, but also for the analysis of the economic situation. The statement has come at the end of the first half of the fiscal year and, therefore, it is helpful to understand the state of the economy at the mid-point of the fiscal year, which is also close to the mid-point of the term of the central government.

On the global economy, the outlook is gloomy. Growth has slowed more than anticipated, trade has contracted more sharply, there is rising protectionism, and 'an uneasy calm prevails on uncertainty about the stance of monetary policy of systemic central banks'.

State of the Economy

On the domestic economy,

- 'the outlook for agricultural activity has brightened;
- the industrial sector has suffered a manufacturing-driven contraction;
- inflation, excluding food and fuel, has been sticky around 5 per

cent, mainly in respect to education, medical and personal care services;

- in the manufacturing sector, the persistence of considerable slack…;
- in the external sector, merchandise exports contracted in the first two months of Q2;
- subdued domestic demand was reflected in a faster contraction in imports;
- the decline in remittances and the flattening of software earnings warrant monitoring;
- while the pace of FDI slowed compared to a year ago, portfolio flows were stronger.'

These conclusions were visible in the numbers that we had read in the last 12 months or more. Let me give only a few figures and say it in a way that is easy to understand:

- In Q1 of 2016–17, GFCF (that is, additional capital investment) *declined* by 3.1 per cent compared to the same period of the previous year.
- In Q1 of 2016–17, net sales of all firms *declined* by 1.9 per cent and of manufacturing firms by 4.8 per cent over Q1 of 2015–16.
- During February–July 2016, credit to all sectors increased by a modest 9.5 per cent, but credit to 'industry' grew by only 1.72 per cent over the same period last year. Credit to micro and small industries *declined* by 3.46 per cent and credit to medium industries *declined* by 10.62 per cent.
- The Index of Industrial Production for all industries during February–July 2016 increased by a mere 0.25 per cent, while for manufacturing it *declined* by 1.01 per cent over the same period last year.
- NPAs of banks stood at 7.6 per cent as against 4.6 per cent at the end of the previous year.

The Ground Reality

Now you know why there is no visible job creation, why there is anxiety among parents, and why there is anger among the youth. Now you know why the job creators (exporters and micro, small and medium industries) have thrown up their hands in despair. Now you know why the large business houses are investing abroad rather than in India.

It is not as if the government is doing nothing right. The government was on the right track when it affirmed its commitment to fiscal consolidation. It is doing the right thing in selling its stake in chronically loss-making public sector enterprises. It is pursuing the right strategy in pushing more investment into infrastructure, especially roads and railways. However, these measures will not be enough unless the private sector—big, medium and small—rediscovers its appetite for investment. That, unfortunately, is not happening.

Poor aggregate demand is the main reason for low investment. That 'doing business in India' has not become easier (despite the hype about climbing a few notches up the ranking ladder) is another crucial reason. Regulators have once again turned into controllers and have churned out reams of rules and regulations that are frightening. Investigating agencies, including the investigation wings of tax departments, have unleashed a wave of threats and terror. Litigation in commercial matters, often involving the government, has reached alarming proportions with no effective alternative dispute resolution mechanism. State governments seem to have lost interest in 'reforms' and seem happier pursuing 'welfarism'.

Government Losing Its Nerve

This is the time when the government should not lose its nerve or its focus. Unfortunately, there are signs that the government is looking for a short-term boost—increase spending to boost growth in the short term and lure the people to be mesmerised by the dazzle of the number 7.6 (of GDP growth).

What else can one make of the government's mandate to a committee to explore the feasibility of 'flexible' fiscal deficit-targeting? And what else can one make of the first sign of 'flexible' inflation-targeting that has emerged out of the statement of the MPC? Why did Governor Urjit Patel push back the deadline for achieving the inflation target from March 2018 to an unspecified medium term?

Both are very bad ideas. I hope the N.K. Singh committee will junk the idea of a flexible fiscal deficit target and recommend that the government should under no circumstances—except in a case of a declared war—breach the limit of 3 per cent for the fiscal deficit. I also hope that in the next policy statement Governor Patel will restore the RBI's stance on inflation and reaffirm that the deadline for achieving the inflation target will remain March 2018.

THE CASE FOR CREATIVE DESTRUCTION

30 October 2016

In my column on 2 October 2016 ('How Free Is Freedom in India?'), I had made a brief reference to the World Bank's Ease of Doing Business Report and concluded thus:

'Despite the reforms since 1991, which is a remarkable story, the State-to-firm interface remains a problem. What needs to be done and what can be done deserve a separate column and I hope to be able to write one soon.'

Accumulated Negligence

The opportunity has come with the publication of the World Bank Group's annual report titled 'Doing Business 2017: Equal Opportunity for All'. The verdict on India is disappointing. In the year between the previous report and the latest, India's overall rank improved one place from 131 to 130 among 190 countries. That means, despite the ambitious goal of getting into the top 50, nothing has changed. It reminds one of the French saying which, in translation, reads, 'The more things change the more they remain the same.' True, India did not reach this depressing position in one year. It is the result of the accumulated mistakes and negligence of the years since Independence, especially the 1960s and 1970s, when the State intervened, massively, in the direction and management of the economy. There was deep distrust of certain institutions (private sector) and natural forces (markets) and there was great dependence on some structures (bureaucracy) and organisations (public sector enterprises). Other key institutions (judiciary, municipal governments) carried on as before, although many parts had become dysfunctional and obsolete.

If one looks closely at the methodology of the study, one could point out significant limitations. As far as India is concerned, it is based on a survey of just two cities—Delhi and Mumbai. Besides, the study is a ranking and measures relative performance among 190 countries; so, even if there is significant improvement on an absolute scale, India's rank may not improve if other countries have done better. Nonetheless, the conclusions are important because they are approximations of the realities of doing business in India.

No Cause for Boasts

The study ranked countries on 10 parameters. In the case of India, there was significant improvement only on two: Getting Electricity (51 to 26) and Enforcing Contracts (178 to 172). There was marginal improvement on two parameters, the rank was the same on one and worsened on the remaining five. Altogether, there is no cause for the boasts that we hear from time to time.

Because of the privatisation of distribution of electricity in Delhi and Mumbai, it is easier to get an electricity connection. Improved supply has also helped. On enforcing contracts, presumably, the courts in Delhi and Mumbai are more aware of the need to be strict although, at 172, the rank is not exactly a badge of honour.

Let's look at the other parameters and consider what can be done.

- **Registering Property (140/138):** Just as we have authorised depositories for securities, we must authorise private registrars who will compete with each other and offer improved and quicker services.
- **Trading across Borders (144/143):** The external environment

has indeed become more protectionist and difficult. So has the environment in India, especially due to the gobbledygook that has found its way back into the Foreign Trade Policy and the Handbook of Procedures. The minister has run out of ideas. It is time for another bonfire, *à la* 1991–92, and a change of guard.

Root and Branch Reforms

- **Starting a Business (151/155):** The obstacles are notorious. Do away with prior permissions in the case of a small or medium business and require the promoter to report the event within 60 days of starting the business.
- **Resolving Insolvency (135/136):** Let the new Insolvency and Bankruptcy Code be tried for a year. Afterwards, it should be brought back to Parliament for amendments that will improve the law.
- **Construction Permits (184/185):** This is the notorious cash generator for municipal authorities everywhere in the world, and India is no exception. I am loath to make any suggestion, but here is one. Introduce public hearing and decision making on the applications. It will be like a hearing in a courtroom and decisions must be handed down on each application at the end of the hearing.
- **Getting Credit (42/44):** With NPAs worsening, it is not surprising that getting credit has become more difficult. To tackle NPAs, the government has relied on threats, arbitrary appointments, and a useless new supervisory board. We had a much worse situation in 1997/1998, and we resolved it through empowering experienced bankers. That is the way to go.
- **Protecting Minority Investors (10/13):** By not filling vacancies for months, the government emasculated the Company Law Board. Now we have the National Company Law Tribunal and the Appellate Tribunal. Their work should be closely monitored so that they deliver results.
- **Paying Taxes (172/172):** Why should *paying* taxes be difficult?

> The BJP coined the phrase 'tax terrorism'. Ask any businessman his view on the current functioning of the Income Tax, Excise and Service Tax Departments, and the phrase you will hear repeatedly is 'tax terrorism'. The recent 'harvest' of ₹65,000 crore of 'black money' and the subsequent actions by different tax authorities have thrown up horror stories. Retrospective tax demands (there was one Vodafone case under the UPA) continue to be made. The government seems to have lost the plot on how to collect taxes and hence I shall offer no suggestion.

I am glad the Prime Minister has called for suggestions on the World Bank Group's report. The best suggestions will be based on 'creative destruction' of the present system.

NO JOBS, NO CREDIT GROWTH, NO PRIVATE INVESTMENTS

27 November 2016

Between the gathering storm on the India-Pakistan border and the massive disruption to the economy, Saturday, 26 November, passed almost unnoticed. The day marked the exact mid-point of the tenure of the government led by Prime Minister Narendra Modi. It is a natural and opportune moment to take stock of the government, its promises, the delivery and the state of the economy.

I made a list of the economic concerns of the average citizen, and then I struck out each concern that was not as important as the remaining concerns. Ultimately, I was left with three and there was no way the list could be pruned further. In my view, the most pressing concerns that are uppermost in everyone's mind are: jobs, credit growth and investment. The past is the view in the rear mirror—noticed but unalterable. The present is represented by the demand for jobs and for credit. The future lies in investments made today and in the following days.

Jobless Growth

'Jobs' is a good starting point. Almost everyone is either employed or self-employed. The employed earn a wage or salary, the self-employed earn an income. The data on jobs created in the last 30 months is stark, revealing and worrying. I cannot do better than quote the words of a former finance minister: 'Fresh job creation continues to suffer and will lose its connect with economic growth.... What is important for us politicians to remember, however, is that the aam aadmi is not concerned with theories. He wants results, and if we fail to provide the people with job opportunities in adequate numbers, they will be disappointed.'

The former finance minister is Mr Yashwant Sinha. His son, Mr Jayant Sinha, was Minister of State for Finance for a little over two years in the present government and is now MoS, Civil Aviation.

Jobless growth has severely dented the claim that the Indian economy is the fastest growing large economy in the world. By one estimate, 15 million persons enter the job market every year. Among Mr Narendra Modi's election promises, the one that attracted millions of young men and women to vote for his party was the promise that he would create 20 million jobs a year. There is empirical evidence that in the last two years, India has witnessed a period of jobless growth.

- Employment generation in eight labour-intensive sectors was 490,000 in 2014 and 135,000 in 2015 compared to 1,250,000 in 2009 (when the Labour Bureau's survey began);
- Contract jobs declined by 21,000 during January–September 2015 compared to an increase of 120,000 during January–September 2014;
- A study by Care Ratings showed that jobs growth was near zero in 2014–15—only about 0.3 per cent;
- Employment generation in manufacturing companies was negative at -5.2 per cent in 2014–15 compared to 3.2 per cent in 2013–14.

Job creation is not easy. According to estimates, 15 million jobs were created during 2005–12, but it still left millions unemployed. The situation has become worse. On jobs, the government has comprehensively failed.

Low Credit Growth

Next, credit growth. Self-employment or job-creation is closely linked to availability of credit. MSMEs (especially micro and small) create the largest number of jobs. The table gives the rate of credit growth in the last three years of the UPA government and the first two years of the NDA government. Apart from other consequences, the immediate impact of low credit growth is lack of new jobs and, in some sectors, loss of jobs. As on 11 November 2016, year-on-year credit growth was just 8.25 per cent. Low credit growth is directly reflected in the index of industrial production (IIP) and in exports. Both IIP and exports are languishing. The government has utterly failed to find an answer to the question why overall rate of credit growth is the lowest rate in 20 years (see table for sectoral growth rates).

Year-on-year Change in Rate of Growth of Credit

Year	*All Industries*	*Micro and Small*	*Medium*	*Large*
2011–12	20.74	12.58	7.53	23.32
2012–13	15.12	20.13	–0.07	15.56
2013–14	12.84	22.48	–0.48	12.25
2014–15	5.61	9.13	–0.32	5.33
2015–16	2.75	–2.24	–7.79	4.24

(in percentage)

Dismal Investments

Lastly, investment. The best measure of investment is growth in GFCF. In 2014–15 and 2015–16, it was 4.85 per cent and 3.89 per cent, respectively, which is low and which is directly reflected in the IIP. The last GDP estimates put out by the CSO show that in Q1 of 2016–17, GFCF shrunk by 3.1 per cent over Q1 of the previous year. According to the Centre for Monitoring of Indian Economy, new private sector project announcements dropped by 21 per cent in July–September 2016 compared to the corresponding quarter in 2015. The growth rate of credit to large industry was 5.33 per cent and 4.24 per cent in the last two years, the lowest in many years (see table). The Finance Minister has repeatedly urged the private sector to invest, but there are no takers either for his exhortation or for bank credit!

So, mid-term, there is no job creation; abysmally low credit growth; and dismal private sector investment. Having failed in the three main subjects, the government claims that it has passed the exam with distinction! Now, you can understand why the Prime Minister chose to dramatically alter the narrative with so-called demonetisation.

UNION BUDGET

The Union Budget is the highlight of the annual economic calendar. I wrote thrice on the subject—pre-budget, on the evening of budget day and post-budget. I predicted correctly that the government would adhere to the path of fiscal consolidation because the price of not doing so would have been too high. The budget for 2016–17 failed the country in many ways—a great opportunity that was wasted—and I did not pull back my punches. The column titled 'Budget 2016–17: The Fiscal Math Is Puzzling' is worth reading more than once. Whether I was right or wrong will be known only when the budget for 2017–18 is presented. By then, of course, the focus would have shifted to the math underlying the new budget!

A WISH LIST AND SOME NOTES OF CAUTION

28 February 2016

It is just as well that the last day of February will fall on a Monday when the budget will be presented. The commentators can pause, take several deep breaths today, and resume their breathless commentary when the dawn breaks tomorrow!

The third budget of any government is a crucial milestone. If the economy is on a roll, it is a time for consolidation; if the economy is stuck, it is the last opportunity to get it unstuck.

The state of the economy is there for all to see:

- Growth is flat—some will say it is overstated—at 7.4 to 7.6 per cent.
- There is acute distress in rural India.
- There is no visible evidence of job creation.
- Two of the four engines of growth—private investment and exports—are sputtering.
- Several projects are stranded or remain stalled.
- The inflation indices are confusing: While the WPI remains negative, CPI has inched upwards to 5.7 per cent in January 2016, leaving both the producers and the consumers unhappy.

No two years will be alike and there are no textbook solutions to the problems faced by the economy. A government must draw upon its imagination and reserves of courage to deal with the economic situation.

Over-Promise, Under-Perform

Mr Narendra Modi's government was voted to office on the promise of rapid and sustained development. If the government had delivered on its promises, everyone should be a little happier today than what he or she was in May 2014. I am afraid I have not come across anyone who is actually happier. On the contrary, everyone, in different degrees, is sulking or sullen. That includes the silent but observant members (especially the seniors) of the ruling establishment who have correctly sensed that there is no wind behind the sails of the government.

The reason is that the government had over-promised but has under-performed. The party (BJP) and its supporters (RSS and its affiliates) did not help the government: they changed the narrative from development to intolerance and from cooperation to confrontation. So, instead of the rise of the economy, we have seen the rise of intolerance. Instead of all sections of the people warming to the government, we find that important sections like farmers, Dalits, tribals, Muslims and students have become apprehensive and insecure.

What should we expect from the budget for 2016–17?

I expect that the Finance Minister will comfortably achieve the fiscal deficit target of 3.9 per cent in the current year. He got a bonanza from low oil prices of approximately ₹140,000 crore that he will use to fill three yawning gaps—shortfall in tax revenues, shortfall in non-tax revenues (especially disinvestment) and the increase in the fiscal deficit. The question is, will he stick to his own fiscal consolidation path and set a target of 3.5 per cent for 2016–17? If he does, we can raise one cheer; if he doesn't, the negative marking will begin.

Distress in Rural India

Secondly, at the top of my 'to-do' list is the acute distress in rural India. There has been a drought or drought-like condition for three years, but the government looked the other way and cut funds of nearly ₹75,000 crore to critical programmes that would have put money into the rural economy. Besides, the government was lukewarm to MGNREGA and did not give reasonable increases in minimum support prices. Rural wages have remained practically stagnant. All these explain the poor demand in the rural economy and the grave unrest among farmers, farm workers and Dalits. We will watch how the budget addresses these issues.

Thirdly, we should look to how the government has balanced its books. Has the government set unrealistic revenue targets or underestimated expenditure?

Fourthly, we should look out for the revised estimates (2015–16) and the budget estimates (2016–17) against key heads of expenditure, particularly the social sector programmes. Will the government meet its expenditure targets in 2015–16 and provide adequate funds for 2016–17?

Fifthly, we will test the budget on how it addresses the problems of sluggish private investment and sputtering exports. A car cannot run on two wheels. So far, the government has remained clueless on the solutions to the twin issues.

Beyond the Numbers

Sixthly, what will be the legislative agenda in 2016–17? Is the government determined to pass the GST Bills and will it accommodate the legitimate views of the Opposition parties? Will the government repeal the retrospective clause in taxation of capital gains? Will the government bring back to the table the Direct Taxes Code and the recommendations of the Financial Sector Legislative Reforms Commission?

Seventhly, will the budget follow the pattern of the last two budgets and make meaningless announcements of ₹50 crore or ₹100 crore each on a clutch of sundry 'initiatives'?

Eighthly, will the government use its absolute majority in the Lok Sabha (not available to any government in the last 30 years) to implement bold structural reforms in the economy, in the regulatory architecture, and in the administrative machinery? I believe that a party that has, on its own, a strength of 282 cannot waste the opportunity or duck the responsibility of making deep and broad structural reforms.

And, finally, we should be curious and ask who wrote the budget speech! My best wishes to the Finance Minister!

IN GOOD TIMES AND BAD TIMES, COURAGE IS THE ALLY

1 March 2016

We can debate endlessly whether these are good times or bad times. Last week, I had pointed out that the economy was facing headwinds. On 26 February, the Economic Survey confirmed my apprehensions. This is what it said in the preface to Volume II Chapter 1: 'Weak growth in advanced and emerging countries has taken its toll on India's exports. As imports have also declined, principally on account of reduced prices of crude oil for which the country is heavily dependent on imports, trade and current account deficits continue to be moderate. Growth in agriculture has slackened due to two successive years of less-than-normal monsoon rains. Saving and investment rates are showing hardly any signs of revival. The rupee has depreciated vis-à-vis the US dollar, like most other currencies in the world, although less so in magnitude… Given the prevalent overall macroeconomic scenario, and assuming a normal level of rains in 2016–17, it would not be unreasonable to conclude that the Indian economy is all set to register growth in excess of 7 per cent for the third year in succession.'

The times are therefore good and bad, and courage is the only ally. Mr Narendra Modi's party (BJP) has a majority (282) in the Lok Sabha and the NDA government has 335 members supporting it. The sun was shining and this was the time to fix the roof. Therefore, on the eve of the budget, I asked, 'Will the government use its absolute majority in the Lok Sabha (not available to any government in the last 30 years) to implement bold structural reforms in the economy, in the regulatory architecture, and in the administrative machinery?' Regrettably, the answer in the budget was in the negative. The government has ducked the responsibility of making deep and broad structural reforms.

Predictions Come True

I had predicted that the government will comfortably achieve the target of fiscal deficit in the current year. It has, and I am happy. I am also happy that the government has spurned the advice of the CEA and stuck to its own fiscal consolidation path for 2016–17. It is a vindication of the UPA government's policy declared after adopting the Vijay Kelkar Committee's report on fiscal consolidation.

At the top of my list I had put the acute distress in rural India. This budget, too, has failed to address the real issues, which are price and productivity. The crucial signal to farmers is 'price'. The government has reneged on its promise to give cost plus 50 per cent. It did worse last year by giving meagre or nil increases in minimum support price (MSP). The budget speech also made no promise of a fair and remunerative MSP. Nor was there any major initiative to increase productivity in crucial crops.

I had also suggested that we should look to how the government has balanced its books. The government boasted that it earned more tax revenues than it had budgeted at the beginning of the year. Did they collect more corporation tax? No. Did they collect more income tax? No. What they collected more was excise duties. It is a whopping increase of ₹54,334 crore! That windfall was due to the numerous times the government increased excise duties on petrol and diesel after the budget was presented last year.

Clueless on Two Issues

The budget was on test on how it addressed the problems of sluggish private investment and sputtering exports. The government remains clueless on the solution to the two issues. While several paragraphs of the speech were devoted to public investment, there was little to encourage or attract private investment. In the core sectors, such as power, steel, coal, mining, cement, construction, and oil and gas, many projects are stranded and there is little new investment. Besides, there is the problem of high interest rates. The budget did not address these issues.

Except for one bland sentence, there was no mention of exports. I think, after 14 successive months of negative growth, the government has given up on the export front.

I had also raised questions on the legislative agenda in 2016–17. The answers were disappointing. In the financial sector, only three proposals of the Financial Sector Legislative Reforms Commission will be taken up for passing legislation. The Direct Taxes Code seems to have been buried permanently. There was only a lukewarm reference to the GST Bills, but there was no promise of accommodating the legitimate criticism of the Opposition.

Taxation sans Philosophy

We may now turn to Part B of the budget speech. The government had promised a predictable tax regime. However, Part B of the speech belied that promise. There was no major relief to the taxpayer or the middle class or the small and medium businessperson. The reduction in the corporate tax rate for a very limited class from 30 to 29 per cent was laughable. Besides, new cesses and surcharges were imposed. Despite having a majority in the Lok Sabha, the government could not summon the courage to repeal the retrospective tax on capital gains (the so-called Vodafone tax). Part B of the speech was a bag of miscellany that did not reveal any philosophy of taxation or tax policy.

Finally, the government wisely refrained from predicting the growth rate for 2016–17. The Economic Survey was restrained in assuming a growth rate of about 7 per cent. The budget papers revealed the GDP estimates for 2015–16 and 2016–17 and calculated the nominal growth at 11 per cent. If these are the government's numbers, how much will the real GDP growth be in 2016–17? We know the RBI's target for inflation in 2016–17 is 4 to 6 per cent. How much does that leave for real growth? It would be a pity that all these elaborate exercises may yield, ultimately, moderate GDP growth of about 6 per cent.

Altogether, I am afraid; the budget has been a wasted opportunity.

DEAR FARMERS—*ACHHE DIN* ARE COMING

6 March 2016

Farmers may rejoice. The government has finally acknowledged that farmers are part of India, that the farm sector faces acute distress, and that farmers need a helping hand. That is something which many commentators—especially Mr Ashok Gulati—have been saying for many months.

Farmers had taken note of the BJP's failure to keep its election promise of offering an MSP of cost plus 50 per cent. I had pointed out that the increases in the MSP in 2015–16 were paltry. Members of Parliament were aghast when Prime Minister Modi declared his contempt for MGNREGA that, according to him, was 'a monument to the failure of the Congress governments'. Critics warned the government that the allocation to MGNREGA was inadequate. Surveys show that farm wages have risen only marginally in 2015–16 adding to the distress.

While the Prime Minister spoke often, and eloquently, on FDI, Make in India and ease of doing business, he paid scant attention to the agriculture sector, leaving it, presumably, to the Minister of Agriculture. The latter, however, was neither seen nor heard and, after nearly 21 months in office, remains largely unknown. [He could take a few lessons from the Minister of Human Resource Development who has acquired a cult status among the 'nationalists and patriots', if not among the students and teachers.]

As a result, the label of *suit-boot ki sarkar* stuck, and something had to be done. I suspect that is how the idea of a 'pro-farmer, pro-rural India budget' was born. Whatever be the motivation, I welcome the government's move to address the problems of the agricultural sector.

Let's Do the Math

It was brave on the part of the Finance Minister to reiterate the Prime Minister's declared goal of 'doubling the income of farmers by 2022'. The budget, we were told, was the first step in this regard. So, what did the budget do?

Let's do the math. Doubling income in six years will mean that the average annual growth rate of farmers' income should be around 12 per cent. Is that possible in a country where 66 per cent of all agricultural land is monsoon-dependent and does not have assured irrigation? Besides, in 2014–15 and 2015–16, the agriculture sector grew at the rate of minus 0.2 per cent and 1.1 per cent, respectively. It is difficult to imagine that the sectoral growth rate will jump to anything close to 12 per cent or farmers' income will grow at 12 per cent per year.

Agricultural income is based on two factors—productivity and price. No one has claimed that there are measures underway to dramatically increase productivity in growing paddy, wheat, sugarcane or pulses in the next six years. Productivity gains in select areas or crops may add about 3 per cent to the farmer's income. That leaves price. Will the government increase the MSP for these crops by 12 per cent per year? There is no clear answer in the budget speech or in the allocations.

Rabbit Out of the Hat

In the speech, there is one possible answer: the total allocation for agriculture and farmers' welfare. It is an impressive jump from ₹15,809 crore in 2015–16 (revised estimates) to ₹35,984 crore (budget estimates) in 2016–17. How did the government manage to pull this rabbit out of the hat? By the simple expedient of shifting the allocation for 'interest subsidy for short-term credit to farmers' from the Department of Financial Services to the Department of Agriculture, Cooperation and Farmers'

Welfare! Minus this shift, the allocations read as follows under the NDA government:

- 2014–15: ₹19,255 crore
- 2015–16 (RE): ₹15,809 crore
- 2016–17 (BE): ₹20,984 crore

Nothing dramatic; the allocation that was cut in 2015–16 has been restored to the level of 2014–15. Allowing for inflation over two years, in real terms, the allocation may be actually less.

The singular idea trotted out as 'path breaking' was the Prime Minister's Fasal Bima Yojana for which an allocation of ₹5,500 crore has been made. The budget documents themselves say that the scheme is basically 'the National Crop Insurance Scheme, which includes existing schemes'. Each of the old schemes was an attempt to make crop insurance better targeted and more effective. It is possible that the Fasal Bima Yojana that rolls all the old schemes into one will be more beneficial to the farmers. I sincerely hope so, but I must say that no new paths have been broken yet.

Non-Farm Income

The way to improve the farmer's income is to improve his non-farm income. Most farmers have no reliable non-farm income except casual manual labour. Non-farm income for a family will be available only if there are jobs outside the farm. Such jobs can be created through public works like road-building, irrigation works and watershed programmes, but they will not be enough. More can be done only through private investments in small, medium and large industries and in the services sector. Such investments have been lacking in the last two years, adding to the distress caused by drought or drought-like conditions in the last three years.

The goal of doubling the income of farmers by 2022 is indeed laudable. Farmers must, however, demand that the government should present a concrete plan to achieve that goal. Otherwise, it will be another *chunavi jumla*.[1]

[1]Election stunt

BUDGET 2016–17: THE FISCAL MATH IS PUZZLING

13 March 2016

The CEA should be glad that he lost the argument on fiscal deficit. It was a good argument to lose! I compliment the Finance Minister for achieving the fiscal deficit target of 3.9 per cent in the current year and fixing a target of 3.5 per cent for 2016–17. That one decision has lent a measure of credibility to the government's professed commitment to the path of reform.

There are, however, questions about the fiscal math of the budget.

Let me go back to my column titled 'Oil Windfall: Gone with the Wind' (10 January 2016). The budget documents have confirmed the initial estimates. The government reaped a windfall of about ₹140,000 crore due to the decline in crude oil prices. The bulk of the gain has been used in the following manner in 2015–16:

- Gap in direct tax receipts: ₹46,000 crore
- Gap in other receipts: ₹44,000 crore
- Lower borrowing due to lower nominal GDP: ₹20,000 crore

A Missed Opportunity

As I had feared, no part of the windfall has been used for additional capital expenditure or socially useful programmes. In fact, total capital expenditure has fallen from ₹241,430 crore in the budget estimates to ₹237,718 crore in the revised estimates for 2015–16.

It was a missed opportunity. If the government had collected its budgeted direct taxes and had achieved its disinvestment target, it could have used a substantial sum for additional capital expenditure. That would have given a big boost to aggregate demand. So, while the government met the fiscal deficit target of 3.9 per cent, it was achieved in an unsatisfactory manner. So, no high marks for fiscal management.

Let us now look at the fiscal deficit target of 3.5 per cent fixed for 2016–17.

Total receipts and total expenditure will be up from ₹1,785,391 crore in 2015–16 (RE) to ₹1,978,060 crore in 2016–17 (BE). That is a huge jump of ₹192,669 crore. Of the total expenditure, ₹533,904 crore will be financed by borrowing (the fiscal deficit), which is about the same level as the borrowing in 2015–16 (₹535,090 crore).

The Fiscal Math Puzzle

How does the government propose to garner additional resources of ₹192,669 crore? This is where the math becomes a puzzle. From the budget documents, the following appear to be the main sources (the numbers have been rounded off):

- Net tax revenue: +₹107,000 crore
- Non-tax revenue: +₹64,000 crore
- Other receipts: +₹31,000 crore

These are ambitious projections of increases in receipts. The assumptions are that direct tax receipts will grow by 12.6 per cent as against 8.3 per cent in 2015–16; spectrum auction will bring in an additional ₹42,000 crore which will boost non-tax revenue; and disinvestment will yield an additional ₹31,000 crore over the level achieved in 2015–16. If these assumptions must be proved to be correct, it will require extraordinary capacity and drive in the Department of Revenue and the Department of

Disinvestment. It will also mean that the telecom service providers will be ready to stake more money for acquiring spectrum.

What is of concern is that, should the assumptions prove to be incorrect, there does not seem to be a Plan B. Will the government cut subsidies or other expenditure? There are already complaints of insufficient allocation to the social sector. Nor is there scope to cut defence expenditure. Perhaps, some payments may be staggered while implementing the Pay Commission report or the One Rank One Pension scheme—both beehives.

The other doubtful part of the fiscal math is the growth of GDP. In 2015–16, nominal GDP grew by 8.6 per cent. The assumption for 2016–17 is that nominal GDP will grow by 11 per cent. The revenue estimates (both tax and non-tax) are crucially dependent on GDP growth. We may keep our fingers crossed.

Off-Budget Borrowings

There is another aspect of the budget that affects the credibility of the fiscal math. These are estimates of borrowing by the Ministry of Railways and the Ministry of Road Transport. Such borrowings, called 'extra budgetary resources (EBRs)', have been kept outside the balance sheet of the government. In the case of Railways, the EBR is projected to jump from ₹48,700 crore in 2015–16 to ₹59,325 crore in 2016–17, and in the case of Road Transport from ₹28,000 crore in 2015–16 to ₹59,279 crore in 2016–17. Apart from the capacity to borrow, the wisdom of such off-budget borrowing is open to question. The correct approach would be for the government to borrow and provide the funds to the two infrastructure ministries in the form of budgetary support. Borrowing large amounts by the two ministries (or their public sector arms) may be unexceptionable in terms of accounting, but is not likely to go down favourably with the eagle-eyed analysts and rating agencies. I shall not be surprised if they will add these extra-budgetary borrowings to the overall fiscal deficit!

The fiscal sum (3.5 per cent) is indeed the right answer, but the fiscal math is puzzling.

TO TALK OR NOT TO TALK

17 January 2016

Barely three weeks ago, Prime Minister Narendra Modi made an unannounced visit to Lahore and agreed with Prime Minister Nawaz Sharif that the two countries will carry forward the agreement on Comprehensive Bilateral Dialogue reached between the two countries. It was hailed as a brave move. Brave or not, it was an unusual, though impulsive, move and helped create an illusion of an atmosphere that would be conducive for talks. The date 15 January was set for talks between the Foreign Secretaries.

Within seven days, terrorists struck at a key frontline facility in India, the Pathankot Air Force base. In February 1999, Prime Minister Vajpayee had visited Lahore and signed the Lahore Declaration with Prime Minister Sharif. Within three months of that visit, in May, the Kargil war began.

Structures within the State

Whoever planned it and whoever executed it, neither the Kargil war nor the Pathankot attack could have been conceived after the visit of the Indian Prime Minister to Lahore. The Indian State is a single entity. There is a structure, there is a command and control and, barring minor aberrations, the State acts and can be commanded to act as a single entity. Pakistan is not. There are at least three structures within Pakistan that exercise 'State' power. There is the federal government of Pakistan, there is the Army, and there is the Inter-Services Intelligence (ISI). No one has control over all the three power structures. The Army and the ISI can act independently, and often do.

At least these three structures are State entities deriving their authority and legitimacy from the written laws of the country. There are others who are, seemingly, beyond the pale of the law. We have coined a quaint phrase to describe them—non-State actors. The most virulent are the Lashkar-e-Toiba (LeT) and the Jaish-e-Muhammed (JeM). They exist in the open, own assets, recruit men and women, threaten jihad against India, proudly claim responsibility for terror attacks, and are seemingly immune from the laws of Pakistan.

This is the reality that India must take into account. A Prime Minister of India, enjoying full authority and responsibility as the true representative of India, cannot assume that the Prime Minister of Pakistan enjoys full authority and responsibility as the true representative of Pakistan. Prime Ministers of India, from Lal Bahadur Shastri to Indira Gandhi and Mr A.B. Vajpayee to Dr Manmohan Singh, have learned that truth to their bitter disappointment. Prime Minister Modi learned it in the months of December and January.

Coming to talks. 'Should India talk to Pakistan?' is the easy question. The answer is 'yes, of course'. The real and difficult questions are who should India talk to, and on what and when? Answers to these questions cannot be found during an impulsive drop-in at a pre-nuptial ceremony, or at a brief pull-aside conversation during a multilateral event. Mr Modi tried to do that, and the ignominious outcome was the terror attack on the Pathankot Air Force base.

Mumbai Is Not Closed, Yet

The Mumbai terror attacks (26–29 November 2008) were the worst terror attacks on Indian soil. It was conclusively proved that the 10 terrorists were Pakistanis; they were trained, armed and despatched from Pakistan; their controllers were located in Pakistan; and the entire operation was guided from Pakistan.

As in every case, including the Kargil war, Pakistan denied that the terrorists were Pakistanis. World opinion forced Pakistan to conduct a perfunctory investigation, make some inconsequential arrests, and start a desultory and mock trial. Eight years later, not one person has been found guilty or punished.

Not counting the numerous intrusions and incidents along the LoC and the international border, Pathankot is the first major terror attack after Mumbai where the source has been traced to Pakistan. Unusual for Pakistan, it has claimed to have started an investigation. The chances are it may go the same way as the so-called investigation into the Mumbai attack. Then what? In fact, it is a shame that no one in the government seems to remember that the earlier investigation and trial have reached a dead-end and have been comprehensively buried.

Talks on What, When?

There is no alternative to talks with Pakistan. So, by all means, let's talk to Pakistan, but we should first talk on matters that are of immediate and grave concern to us—not respecting the LoC and the international border, terrorism, intrusions, covert support to Indian jihadis, etc. We can also talk on issues that will promote the economic interests of India such as trade, tourism and visits of academics and scholars. But, in my view, we must draw a red line: No talks, for the present, on Kashmir or Siachen or Sir Creek. Nothing will be lost if India maintains the status quo on those issues for some more time.

Pakistan is not a rogue State, but it harbours and covertly supports rogue elements. While war is not the answer, hard or coercive diplomacy could be. India has been forced to defer the Foreign Secretary-level talks to an undetermined date. The time between now and that date must be used to re-examine all aspects of the talks—when, where and on what subjects. These are matters where we must assert our right to exercise our choice.

LIFT THE VEIL, HOLD A DEBATE

4 September 2016

Last week, India and the United States quietly signed the Logistics Exchange Memorandum of Agreement (LEMOA). The agreement had been under discussion since 2002. NDA I and the UPA governments, especially the Ministry of Defence under Mr A.K. Antony, were not in favour. The Congress party too had reservations. The Left parties stoutly opposed the proposal. The discussions dragged on.

The US laid stress on the fact that it had signed the Logistics Support Agreement (LSA) with a hundred countries. What has been signed between India and the US is not the LSA, but a modified version called LEMOA. Obviously, both sides have yielded to each other's concerns.

The agreement has not been made public. We have only a press release and some comments made by the Minister of Defence, Mr Manohar Parrikar, and his counterpart, Mr Ashton Carter. Both were at pains to emphasise that the agreement was not a 'military pact'.

Who Needs Whom More

At present, we can draw our conclusions, preliminary of course, only on the basis of the press release. The agreement is in two parts: one part deals with obligations that have been agreed upon and the other part deals with obligations that may be undertaken on a case-by-case basis.

There are five situations in which both sides are obliged to provide logistics support. They are:

- authorised port visits,
- joint exercises,
- joint training,
- humanitarian assistance and
- disaster relief.

The question is how likely is it that India will call upon the US to provide logistics support? How often is an Indian long-range vessel (we have one aircraft carrier) likely to visit a US port? How often is an Indian Air Force (IAF) aircraft likely to operate far beyond Indian bases, and why would they do so? As far as humanitarian assistance or disaster relief is concerned, are Indian personnel likely to be deployed in the Americas or Europe? In my view, Indian defence forces are not likely to be deployed in any theatre, even in peacetime, beyond our borders with Pakistan, China, Nepal, Bangladesh and Myanmar—at best, they may go near Sri Lanka or Maldives. In any of those situations, there is little or nothing that the US can offer in terms of logistics support under the agreement.

On the other hand, the US is more likely to need India's port services and logistics support. The US's theatres of operation are all over the world, including the Middle East, Asia-Pacific region and the South China Sea. US vessels and aircraft are routinely deployed in these theatres for reconnaissance, surveillance and sometimes even as a deterrent operation.

Only time will tell which side calls upon the other side to provide logistics support and how often. That the US has entered into one hundred such agreements and India has signed its first such agreement is sufficient indication of who needs it more!

A Significant Shift?

The definition of logistics support is unexceptionable, but it is the unexceptionable that sometimes becomes the unthinkable. 'Logistics Support, Supplies and Services' is defined to include food, water, billeting, transportation, petroleum, oils, lubricants, clothing, communication services, medical services, storage services, training services, spare parts and components, repair and maintenance services, calibration services and port services. On the face of it, there is nothing wrong with that list. How will it be applied in practice is the million dollar question.

Take, for example, 'billeting'. The dictionary meaning of the word is 'a place where troops are lodged'. Then there are services like communication services, storage services, training services, repair and maintenance services and calibration services. Will US troops be lodged in India? Is it likely that the logistics services will be allowed to be provided by Indians to the US defence services such as warships, combat aircraft, US Marines or Navy Seals? Will not the US demand that Americans (usually defence personnel) be allowed to enter India to provide these services to their men and equipment? If that happens, will it not be the first time that India would have allowed foreign defence personnel to be stationed on Indian soil (maybe temporarily)?

The other part of the agreement is the 'may be undertaken' part. According to the press release, 'Logistics support for any other cooperative efforts shall only be provided on a case-by-case basis.' So far, so good, but the two countries appear to have tacitly agreed to enlarge the cooperation between the defence forces of the two countries.

More Than a Handshake

Sure, LEMOA is not a military pact. Nevertheless, it is a fair conclusion that it is more than a handshake between the two countries. They have embraced each other! The world is watching, especially Russia, which has been our main supplier so far, and China. LEMOA will certainly be seen as an Indian endorsement of the US policy of 'pivot to Asia'.

That is why editorials and commentators have cautioned that enhanced defence cooperation—following the designation of India by the US as a 'major defence partner'—should not affect India's strategic military neutrality or ability to pursue an independent foreign policy. The exhortations are valid because the US is keen to sign two more 'foundational agreements'—the Communications Interoperability and Security Memorandum of Agreement and the Basic Exchange and Cooperation Agreement.

If the government believes that LEMOA is indeed reciprocal—not merely in its words, but in the benefits that will accrue to both countries—it should make the document public and invite a public debate.

IN SEARCH OF A PAKISTAN POLICY

25 September 2016

It is said that 'Hard words break no bones'. But words have a way of coming back to haunt the speaker.

I am prepared to allow much latitude for a leader who had never been a minister in the central government and was, by his own admission, an outsider so far as Delhi and the central government were concerned. Even so, the language that Mr Narendra Modi had used against Pakistan, when leading the campaign for the BJP in the Lok Sabha election, was unusually belligerent. It revealed a man who had not reflected on the choice and the consequences of his words.

Feeling the Heat

Prime Minister Modi is feeling the heat now. According to a survey/poll, by an overwhelming majority, the 'people' want India to use maximum military force against Pakistan. Cheerleaders among the media unabashedly declared that 'India wants revenge' and 'India wants retribution'. A general secretary of the BJP (on loan from the RSS) proclaimed the doctrine of 'for one tooth, the whole jaw'. Most Indians, according to the survey/poll, did not approve of the way the Modi government had handled the situation in the wake of the Pathankot and Uri terror attacks.

The Prime Minister said that the perpetrators of the Uri terror attack 'will not go unpunished'. Juxtaposed with what Mr Modi had said in the run-up to the election in 2014, it was not unfair to interpret his statement to mean that India will use military force to hit back at Pakistan.

As I write this column, five days after the Uri terror attack, there has been no military action. There was an unverified claim of the Army killing some infiltrators (and losing a jawan). The Ministry of External Affairs stirred itself to action in words—strongly worded statements, a scolding to the High Commissioner of Pakistan and a stinging rebuttal at the United Nations.

It is *déjà vu*. We have gone through this ritual before. There is a terror attack, the evidence points to Pakistan as the source, there are indignant voices and calls for retribution, saner voices advise a measured approach, the limits of India's capacity are grudgingly acknowledged, and India finally settles for a diplomatic offensive. This may appear to be a loser's rationalisation, but it is not.

Pakistan Today

The best deterrent against terror attacks emanating from Pakistan is a coherent and consistent policy towards Pakistan, the main elements of which ought to follow from the recognition that:

1. Pakistan is not a stable country under one government; there are many structures within Pakistan that enjoy governmental powers, notably the Army and the ISI. There are also many non-State actors who have a free run and the blessings of State actors.
2. The internal security situation in Pakistan is brittle. There is unrest in many provinces.
3. Pakistan's economy is fragile and on the brink of failure. The federal government has little support among the people and is desperate to drum up support through diversionary actions.
4. Pakistan is ruled by a narrow elite class that has captured the positions of authority in the bureaucracy and the defence forces. The politicians—also largely from the same narrow elite class—have no

alternative but to join hands with their compatriots in the bureaucracy and the defence establishment.

5. Islamist forces, if not the Islamic State itself, have gained strength in Pakistan in the last decade.

The UPA government's policy towards Pakistan was an attempt to recognise these elements and forge a policy that would safeguard the territory of India, secure the country against terror attacks, and deter Pakistan from embarking upon any misadventure in J&K. It was not a perfect policy, there were a few missteps but, by and large, we achieved our objectives.

There was no war between India and Pakistan; the last war was fought over Kargil in 1999. There was no freeze in the relationship; India and Pakistan continued to engage with each other at different levels without exuberant gestures (singing 'Happy birthday to you' at Lahore) or imperious cancellations (on the eve of the Foreign Secretary-level talks).

After the Mumbai terror attack, there was no terror attack between 2008 and 2014 whose source could be traced to Pakistan. There was no *fidayeen* attack between January 2010 and March 2013. In short, Pakistan behaved. The situation in the Kashmir valley improved dramatically after 2010 and there was a boom in tourist arrivals. The years between 2010 and 2014 witnessed the lowest number of casualties among civilians and security forces.

Defensive–Offensive

Wisdom lies in bringing hard analysis, cold logic, pragmatism and self-interest to crafting a Pakistan policy. We must learn lessons from the past: Kargil, Agra, Sharm el-Sheikh, Mumbai, Lahore/Pathankot and Uri. Under the circumstances, a defensive–offensive policy seems to be the best policy.

That means we must first take measures on our side to strengthen border security, prevent infiltration, increase our intelligence assets, and take pre-emptive action, wherever possible.

That means we must engage Pakistan at different levels, but keep a deliberate and cautious distance.

That means we must acknowledge that there is an unresolved political issue in J&K and take bold, out-of-the-box initiatives to find an honourable and constitutional solution through dialogue with the stakeholders in J&K.

And, in this game of chess, that means not succumbing to hubris (when we make an important gain) or to despondency (when we suffer a temporary setback).

WAKE UP AND SMELL THE COFFEE

23 October 2016

Even by the usual standards it was a l-o-n-g communique consisting of 109 paragraphs, each marked not by a number, but by a bullet point. I can imagine what would have happened when the deputies gathered to draft the communique. I am reminded of how a camel was created: the Creator appointed a committee to design a horse and when the Creator breathed life into the design, a camel was born!

Communiques are long in the making but have a short life. A communique is only good up to the time of the next communique. The principals (Presidents and Prime Ministers) spend little time on the communique. It is a rare occasion when one country/leader will invest a lot of time, diplomatic effort and personal goodwill in persuading other countries/leaders to highlight a certain matter in the communique. The Goa summit of BRICS countries promised to be one such rare occasion.

India's Main Concern

In the days preceding the summit, India was preoccupied with one subject: Pakistan-sponsored terrorism. Ever since the cross-LoC action on 29 September 2016, the government (especially the Defence Minister) and the BJP were determined to extract as much political advantage as possible from an Army operation that was accurately described by the Foreign Secretary as 'target-specific, limited-calibre, counter terrorist operation'. The government did extract mileage in India and hoped to do the same when India was in a gathering that represented 43 per cent of the world's population.

The Prime Minister churned out some devastating words and phrases. He said Pakistan 'embraces and radiates the darkness of terrorism'. He also said terrorism had become Pakistan's 'favourite child'. In another speech, he said Pakistan is the 'mothership of terrorism'.

Expectations from the summit were, therefore, high. We believed that Pakistan will be isolated, named and shamed, and Pakistan will be banished to join North Korea as an outlaw. We believed that the JeM will be named, deservedly, after the Uri terror attack and the LeT will be named because it was the perpetrator of the Mumbai terror attack (2008).

Disappointing Communique

When the BRICS communique was released, we scoured the paragraphs to find the reference to Pakistan. There was none. We blinked, read the communique again, but there was no reference. We looked for a reference to the Uri attack and words of sympathy for India. Again, none. All that we found, buried in paragraph 57, were the following words:

'We strongly condemn the recent several attacks, against some BRICS countries, including that in India.'

What was the meaning of the word 'that'? Was it a grudging reference to the Uri attack? No one has bothered to explain to the people of India the non-reference to Uri when the summit took place in India within a month of the Uri attack that left 19 soldiers dead.

There was more. Two paragraphs below there was a message to the world, India included:

'All counter terrorism measures should uphold international law and respect human rights.'

Counterterrorism measures are taken by countries that are the victims of terrorist attacks. India's recent cross-LoC action was one such measure. Did the communique imply that India had violated international law? Did it imply that India did not respect human rights?

Self-Interest Prevails

While there was no reference to the Uri attack and no reference to Pakistan or the JeM or the LeT, the communique named a notorious terror group: the Islamist State in Iraq and the Levant (ISIL). Only one other terrorist group, the Jabhat al-Nusra (in Syria), was named. The references were not accidental. Both Russia and China feel threatened by ISIL (also known as ISIS). Russia has a special interest in Syria. Hence, the naming of ISIL and Jabhat al-Nusra. For the same reasons, Russia and China need the support of Pakistan.

Last month, Russia concluded a military exercise with Pakistan. At the United Nations, China blocked India's efforts to name Masood Azhar as a terrorist and put curbs on his activities. After the BRICS summit, China went a step further and, in the unkindest cut of all, China's spokesperson said, 'Everyone knows that India and Pakistan are victims of terrorism. Pakistan has made huge efforts and great sacrifices in fighting terrorism. I think that the international community should respect this.' That is the real world. The real world fears an escalation of a conflict between two countries that have nuclear weapons and, therefore, is unwilling to pour oil on the fire. Besides, each country has its self-interest to protect. For Russia, it is the situation in Afghanistan and the ISIS's threat to its territory via Uzbekistan, Turkmenistan and Kyrgyzstan. For China, it is its investments in Pakistan, the Road and Belt initiative and access to Gwadar port.

That is not to suggest that India is friendless in the world. It is only to emphasise that, despite the government's efforts, Pakistan is also not friendless in the world. After the Uri attack, the government did the right thing in allowing the Army to take cross-LoC action. The Army also did the right thing in making a measured statement through the DGMO. Message conveyed, the line should have been drawn there. It was not, and expectations of support were built high; hence, the feeling among the people of India of being let down by our BRICS partners.

At least now the government should tacitly acknowledge the wisdom of 'strategic restraint'. It is time to end the rhetoric and the celebrations and go back to deterrence, diplomacy, engagement and talks.

NEW NOTES FOR OLD IS NOT A GAME CHANGER

13 November 2016

Money, inherently, has no colour. In most countries, specified money transactions are taxed. This gives rise to two classes of money—money that is not taxed and money that is taxed. If money that is liable to be taxed is not offered to tax or otherwise escapes taxation, that money is usually referred to as unaccounted money or 'black money'.

The best known tax on money is income tax. It is regarded as a progressive tax—more the income, more the tax. Not many are happy to pay income tax. They view income tax rates as excessive and income tax as confiscatory.

Non-Taxable Income

The tax evader is regarded as a villain. Sometimes, wrong persons are dubbed as villains. If, for policy reasons, a significant part of the incomes earned by the people is not taxed, those incomes are perfectly legal and legitimate. The best example is India where agricultural income is not taxed, but is legitimate and legal income.

As long as taxable income and non-taxable income coexist, when money passes from one person to another, it may change colour. Consider money passing from a farmer to a shopkeeper to a doctor. Depending upon who is a taxable entity, it may turn from white to black and to white again.

Besides, as any economist will point out, black money is not entirely 'stock'. Mostly, it is a 'flow'. In the old days, perhaps unaccounted money was stored as cash—the proverbial 'under the mattress'. Nowadays, unaccounted money is mostly hidden in real estate, buildings, bullion, jewellery and shares/securities. All of the above make it difficult to stop the generation of unaccounted money and it is also difficult to detect the flow of unaccounted money.

Not Demonetisation

A few days ago, the government announced that currency notes of the denomination of ₹500 and ₹1,000 had been 'demonetised'. 'Demonetisation' has a special meaning. It means that the currency note of that denomination will, henceforth, be a scrap of paper! Nothing of that kind happened.

The government's notification of 8 November 2016 withdrew the 'legal tender status' from the notes of the two denominations, but made it clear that those 'holding these notes can tender them at any office of the RBI or any bank branch and obtain value thereof by credit to their accounts'. So, we can be clear on one thing, there was no demonetisation, and the government's spokespersons would be well advised to avoid that word. The correct way to describe the decision is 'new notes for old'!

Both the government and the RBI have declared three objectives for the 'new notes for old' decision. Firstly, to 'tackle counterfeiting Indian banknotes'. This is nothing new, the RBI does this from time to time, new series notes are issued and the old series notes are impounded over a period of time and destroyed. The second objective is to 'curb funding of terrorism through fake notes'. This is really a part of the first objective. The third objective is to 'nullify black money hoarded in cash'. The assumption is that unaccounted money is stored in ₹500 and ₹1,000 notes and, therefore, they must be 'nullified'.

At the end of March 2016, there were 1,570 crore ₹500 notes and 632 crore ₹1,000 notes in circulation, representing 86 per cent, by value, of all notes in circulation. True demonetisation required two steps. Step one: pull out the demonetised notes by forcing people to deposit them in banks within a 51-day period ending on 30 December. Step two: destroy the notes. For obvious reasons, the government did not dare to take the second step—it would have started a revolution!

The reality is the old notes if tendered will be replaced by new notes. Hence, the true test will be the answer to the question: 'What proportion of the old notes will be tendered for replacement'? It is only the notes that are not tendered that will be 'demonetised' in the true sense of the word.

Put on the Thinking Cap

There are many uncertainties and unknowns in the government's plan:

1. How did the government come to the conclusion that the ₹500 note was, in the present day, a high denomination note?
2. Was the government prepared to handle the demand for new notes? The first few days have been utterly chaotic and people have been put through a lot of hardship.
3. What will be the cost of replacing the old notes with new notes, including the cost of printing the new notes? My estimate is ₹15,000 to ₹20,000 crore. Was the cost worth the effort?
4. The present cash to GDP ratio is 12 per cent. Will it come down to the world average of about 4 per cent?
5. The value of the high denomination notes currently in circulation is about 15 lakh crore rupees. Will that value come down significantly?
6. Will gold imports surge indicating that unaccounted income/wealth will seek refuge in bullion and gold jewellery?
7. How will the government's plan stop the generation of fresh black money?
8. And the most puzzling aspect: how will the government's objectives

be met if new and higher denomination series of notes (₹2,000) are introduced?

I have been derisively referred to as a columnist. Will the bloggers, if not the ministers, please answer the questions of this columnist?

DEMONETISING NOTES OR DEMONISING CASH?

20 November 2016

I am obliged to return to the subject of 'New Notes for Old' because the hardship and suffering of the people continue. It is now clear that the decision to demonetise notes of ₹500 and ₹1,000 was ill-conceived, the preparation was terrible and the implementation was horrible. It has also emerged, through whispers of course, that besides the Prime Minister, no more than four officials were in the loop, and the CEA was not among those!

Horrendous Consequences: Look at the Disruption

1. About 86 per cent of the currency in circulation was declared 'illegal tender' in one fell swoop, leaving practically no money with millions of people. There was no money to buy milk or medicines, pay for an auto or taxi, or buy vegetables or grain. I know people who went without a meal for a whole day because no eatery would accept a ₹500 note.
2. There are 134,000 branches of banks in the country. Add 215,000 ATMs of which about 40 per cent were working. Assuming that 500 persons, on average, stood in line outside each branch or ATM, every

day more than 11 crore people spent hours standing in a queue to exchange notes. Most of them were working people. Calculate the impact on production and productivity.

3. For some inexplicable reason, district cooperative banks were not allowed to exchange the notes. Millions of farmers could not deposit or withdraw money and, in the sowing season, there was no money to buy seeds or fertilisers or hire labour.
4. Wholesale markets shut down. Weekly fairs stopped. Retail outlets reported a calamitous fall in sales.
5. Industrial hubs such as Tiruppur, Surat, Ichalkaranji, etc., ground to a halt because there was no money to pay wages to the workers and no money to pay for ancillary and support services like transport.
6. About 33 per cent of all employed persons are casual labourers (estimated at 15 crore). Suddenly, they found themselves without work because those who employed them could not find the money to pay wages.
7. Brokers and touts sprung up offering to exchange the 'demonetised' notes for a price. Men and women, without regular work, offered to stand in line to exchange notes for a fee. Honest people turned dishonest to get some money. The government's response was to use indelible ink to mark the finger. It could have added a voting machine and converted each bank branch and ATM into a polling station!

Ignorant Boasts

The pain and suffering will continue because it will take months to print notes of the new series to replace the 2,300 crore notes of old series and because of the limitations of bank staff and the ATMs (yet to be recalibrated). Meanwhile, the boasts of the government will unravel:

- **Will Demonetisation End Bribery?** Of course, not. Those who will take bribes will take them in the new notes. A case of bribery was reported from Gujarat where two officials of the Kandla Port Trust were caught receiving 124 notes of ₹2,000!

- **Will It Stop Counterfeiting?** Of course, not. If one human can print notes with new security features, another human can find a way to copy those features. The most counterfeited currency in the world is the US dollar. One way to combat counterfeiting is to phase out, periodically, old series of notes and introduce new series and try to stay one step ahead. The last time we did that was in January 2014.
- **Will It Plug Generation of Black Money?** Of course, not. Sectors which are prone to use unaccounted money (wholesale trade, construction, jewellery, higher education, election funding, etc.) will continue to demand unaccounted money and, therefore, ways will be found to supply unaccounted money.

No major economy is entirely free from the scourge of a black or shadow economy. According to a World Bank study, the shadow economy in the US is 8.6 per cent of GDP (or about $1,600 billion), in China 12.7 per cent (about $1,400 billion) and in Japan 11 per cent (about $480 billion). India's shadow economy is estimated to be $500 billion (22.2 per cent of its GDP of $2,250 billion). It is large, but not unusual, and the good news is that its size is shrinking. Brazil, Russia and South Africa have larger shadow economies; Israel and Belgium are comparable.

Demonising Cash

The Prime Minister seems to have bought the idea of a cashless economy and decided to wage a war on cash. His supporters called it a 'surgical strike', little realising that the bulk of the money transactions of the people of India are legitimate and in cash—and will be in cash for a long time—for many reasons. Let me share one crucial data point: for 133 crore people, at the retail level, there are only 1,460,000 Points of Sale (PoS)! Cash to digital is a long journey.

The 'surgical strike' post-Uri was intended to put an end to infiltrations, but the reality is that there has been a threefold jump in infiltrations (as admitted by the government). The 'surgical strike' on currency has resulted in the immiserisation of millions of people and bringing many sectors of the economy to a grinding halt. I shudder to think what the next 'surgical strike' will be and what dreadful consequences that will bring.

MONUMENTAL MISMANAGEMENT

4 December 2016

Dr Manmohan Singh is a man of few words. He speaks softly and is careful not to offend anyone. These, in my view, are excellent attributes of a leader but, in a loud and raucous democracy, they are regarded as failings. Our democracy is poorer for encouraging lung power. Our debates are poorer because fact and logic are overwhelmed by falsehood and rhetoric.

Dr Singh spoke in the Rajya Sabha on Thursday, 24 November 2016. He spoke for barely seven minutes, softly, haltingly, almost apologetically for intruding into the business of the House! He said that in the implementation of the decision to demonetise currency notes, the government was guilty of 'monumental mismanagement'.

The Prime Minister was present but, inexplicably, did not choose to respond.

However kind the media may be to the government (some sections have been disgustingly indulgent and unctuous), they were obliged to report Dr Singh's remarks. So, the words 'monumental mismanagement' were played over and over again on television and were repeated in the social and print media. They have left an indelible impression in the minds of the people.

Signature Tune

'Monumental mismanagement' seems to be the signature tune of the NDA government. Any challenge that they take up ends up more complex and dangerous than before. Demonetisation is the latest example. It is now clear, by putting together private first-person accounts and the movement of the persons concerned, that only four officials had been taken into confidence and tasked to carry out demonetisation. None of them had sufficient knowledge of currency production and management and, therefore, none of the following critical questions was asked or answered:

1. How many discrete currency notes will cease to be legal tender on the midnight of 8–9 November 2016?
   Ans: 2,300 crore notes.
2. What is the capacity of the government's and RBI's printing presses?
   Ans: 300 crore notes per month.
3. How long will it take to replace the demonetised notes by new notes?
   Ans: If we replace note for like note, it will take seven months. If we replace a 500-rupee note by a 100-rupee note, it will take five times longer. If we print more 2,000-rupee notes, the time will be shorter.

Bizarre Decision

4. Is there a justification to introduce 2,000-rupee notes?
   Ans: None at all. If the problems of corruption and black money stem from high denomination notes and, hence, 500- and 1,000-rupee notes will be demonetised, there is absolutely no case for introducing a higher denomination note.
5. Can the new notes be distributed through ATMs immediately?
   Ans: No. The ATMs have to be recalibrated to stack and dispense the new 2,000- and 500-rupee notes. Recalibrating 215,000 ATMs will need a month, perhaps more.
6. So, how will the new notes be distributed quickly?

Ans: They cannot be distributed quickly because of limitations of bank branches and bank staff.

7. Will there be a currency shortage and for how long?

   Ans: There will be an acute currency shortage and it will last for a long time. Apart from the limitations mentioned above, the more crucial factor is the skewed distribution of bank branches and ATMs:

   a. Bank Branches (Total: 138,626)
      - Two-thirds are located in metro, urban and semi-urban areas.
      - Only about a third (47,443) are in rural areas and the distance to the nearest branch could be several kilometres.

   b. ATMs (Total: 215,000)
      - 55,690 ATMs are located in the seven metro cities.
      - 90 per cent of all ATMs are located in 16 states.
      - Only 10 per cent of all ATMs (21,810) are located in 13 states and 7 Union Territories.
      - The seven states in the northeast have only 5,199 ATMs, of which 3,645 are in Assam.

Cost to Economy

8. What will be the cost of demonetisation to the economy?

   Ans: The cost will be significant. Assume, conservatively, that the GDP will drop by 1 per cent. According to the budget papers, the size of the GDP at the end of 2016–17 will be about ₹150 lakh crore. One per cent of that will be ₹1.5 lakh crore.

The CMIE has calculated the cost of demonetisation for the 50-day period from 8 November to 30 December as ₹128,000 crore:

- Households (queuing, transaction cost): ₹15,000 crore
- Government and RBI (printing): ₹16,800 crore
- Business (loss of business, sales): ₹61,500 crore
- Banks (staff cost): ₹35,100 crore

9. How much of the demonetised currency will return to the system

through exchange of notes or deposits?

Ans: The total value of the demonetised notes as on 31 March was ₹1,417,000 crore. If 90 per cent of the notes, by value, return to the system, the 'effective' demonetisation will be only ₹140,000 crore, that will be more than wiped out by the loss of GDP. (As on 27 November, ₹844,982 crore, by value of notes, had been exchanged or deposited. My sources tell me that over ₹1,100,000 crore had been deposited until 2 December. If deposits will be made at the same rate over the next four weeks, the notes that could return to the system may exceed 90 per cent of the demonetised notes!)

10. If it is possible that nearly all the 'demonetised' notes could return to the system, why should we do this exercise?

    Ans: Because, sometimes a government amuses itself with *khoda pahad nikli chuhia*![1]

[1]Digging a mountain and finding a rat.

THE UNRAVELLING

11 December 2016

The phrase of the year 2016, at least as far as India is concerned, was 'surgical strike'. The Oxford Dictionary's word of the year, 'post-truth', was largely unknown to Indians. I confess that I had not heard the word used in conversations or lectures before it was declared as the word of the year.

Surgical strike is simple, easy to understand and, above all, indicates that brain and brawn have combined to produce results. It also hints at qualities such as team work, meticulous preparation, precise execution, desired outcomes and success. Although I bristled when the phrase was first used officially to describe the cross-border action on 29 September 2016, I had to grudgingly acknowledge that the choice of phrase was politically astute.

Unfortunately, a cross-border action is anything but a surgical strike. It serves to restore balance between two border guarding forces that stare at each other night and day, but does no more. It inflicts few casualties on the enemy. There is no damage to vital military assets. It does not alter the status quo. The Indian Army knows this, yet, for some reason, they played along when the government—and especially the Defence Minister—went to town crowing about the surgical strike that would teach a lesson to, and put an end to all infiltrations from, Pakistan.

Has Anything Changed?

The year 2016 began with a terrorist attack on an Air Force base at Pathankot. Since then, there have been more attacks:

- 2 January: Air Force Station, Pathankot
- 18 September: Brigade Headquarters, Uri
- 29 September: 'Surgical strike'
- 2 October: Battalion Headquarters, Rashtriya Rifles, Baramulla
- 29 November: Corps Headquarters, Northern Command, Nagrota

There is a pattern. The targets are military establishments. A small number of *fidayeen* carry out the attack. They infiltrate at night and carry out the attack in the early hours of the morning. They are able to penetrate the perimeter security. The *fidayeen* are prepared to die. In J&K, the situation on the ground is worse than it was last year. Until 5 December 2016, the comparative picture of deaths was the following:

	2015	*2016*
Militants	108	146
Security forces	39	81
Civilians	22	17

Surgical Strike on Cash

As the surgical strike across the LoC was unravelling, there was another on 8 November 2016. This time it was on currency notes of the denomination of ₹500 and ₹1,000. It was a strike, as proclaimed, to end counterfeiting, terrorist funding, and black money and corruption. The 'inconvenience' to the people was to last a few days. The expected 'gain' was huge: apart from putting an end to black money, etc., the government expected to get a bonanza of ₹300,000 crore in the form of a special dividend from the RBI.

As it turns out, the surgical strike on cash has unravelled faster—in less than a month. The queues outside banks and ATMs are still long, banks run out of cash within a few hours of opening, and most ATMs are dry and non-functional. All major markets remain closed or severely crippled. Retail business is down by as much as 80 per cent. Farmers have no cash to buy seeds or fertilisers or hire labour. Millions of people have been deprived of their daily wage or income for a month.

The unkindest cut—for the government—has been the virtual admission by the Revenue Secretary (and by the Vice-Chairman, NITI Aayog) that nearly all the demonetised notes may be returned to the banking system! He did deny and clarify, but the correspondent stuck to his guns and quoted his exact words. If nearly all of the ₹1,544,000 crore, by value, of the demonetised notes will be deposited in banks and post offices, why did the government embark upon this ill-conceived adventure that has severely dented the economy and affected the lives of millions of people?

No Objective Achieved

Has the surgical strike on cash ended black money? There were at least two big, fat weddings recently and, presumably, they were conducted on shoestring budgets! Huge caches of new ₹2,000 notes have been seized from many persons (₹10 crore in Tamil Nadu!).

Has the surgical strike ended terrorist funding? New ₹2,000 notes were found on the bodies of two terrorists killed in an encounter in Bandipora on 22 November.

Has the surgical strike ended corruption? Within days of demonetisation, arrests were made for giving and taking bribes—in new ₹2,000 notes—in Maharashtra, Gujarat, Andhra Pradesh, Odisha, West Bengal and Karnataka!

Has the surgical strike ended counterfeiting? Wait for a while, and the first fake ₹2,000 note will surface.

Has the surgical strike got a bonanza for the government? The RBI put an end to that pipe dream when, on 7 November, the Governor said: 'The withdrawal of legal tender status does not extinguish any of the RBI's balance sheet (liabilities). And, therefore, there is no implication on the balance sheet as of now.' Asked if the RBI would transfer its gain to the government, Mr Patel said, 'That question does not arise as of now.' After he said that, he dealt a final blow by lowering the estimate of GDP growth in 2016–17 from 7.6 per cent to 7.1 per cent!

This is not how 2016 was supposed to end: a grave situation on the border and mounting casualties, immiserisation of the poor, and a severe blow to economic growth. The government claims there will be a 'new normal'. Many will believe that the 'old normal' was better.

WINNERS, LOSERS AND THOSE RUINED

18 December 2016

This week too, I must stay with the subject of demonetisation.

When change takes place, there will be winners and losers. Wisdom is required to cap the gains of the winners and limit the losses of the losers. Greater wisdom is required to ensure that no one is utterly ruined. Such wisdom can only come from full information and knowledge.

Piecing together bits of evidence that are freely available in Delhi—especially from the government and BJP sources—it is now absolutely clear that the Prime Minister was not told:

1. That demonetising ₹500 and ₹1,000 notes will result in 86 per cent, by value, of all currency notes being withdrawn from circulation and use.
2. That printing capacity is limited and replacing the demonetised notes (2,400 crore in number) will take seven months, if every note is replaced by a note of the same denomination; more time if a note is replaced by smaller denomination notes; and less time if the notes are replaced by ₹2,000 notes.
3. That it will take a month or more to recalibrate the 215,000 ATMs and stack them with the new notes (if sufficient notes are supplied).

Skeletons Tumbling Out

Without full information, and without asking the right questions, the Prime Minister unilaterally took the decision to demonetise high denomination notes (₹500 and ₹1,000). His confident demeanour and rhetoric swayed the people. The vast majority believed him when he said that demonetisation will stamp out black money, corruption, fake currency notes and terrorist funding. They believed him when he said that the inconvenience will be short-lived (his Finance Minister even fixed the following Tuesday [15 November] as the day on which things would become normal!). They believed him when he asked for forbearance for 50 days. They stood patiently in long lines, for long hours, and did not protest too much even if they returned empty-handed.

Until last week, the Prime Minister had the upper hand. Then, the skeletons started to tumble out of the cupboard. Every promise of the government turned out to be hollow and false. The myth around demonetisation began to unravel. The winners and losers were identified. And we found to our shock that the lives of millions had been utterly ruined.

Winners and Losers

Who are the winners? The hoarders who laundered every note in their hoard. The launderers and brokers who earned huge commissions. The bank officers who converted the demonetised notes and handed over bundles of new ₹2,000 notes to tax evaders and corrupt officials. The petty government officials, including policemen, who cajoled or threatened bank officials to open a back door exchange counter to exchange old notes for new. Together, they have succeeded beyond imagination and practically ensured that every rupee of the ₹1,544,000 crore will be returned to the banking system!

Who are the losers? The average person who was compelled to make several visits to the bank to withdraw money from his own account. The person with a few old notes who had no access to a bank branch (because of distance) and exchanged her notes at a discount. The homemaker who had to scrounge for money to provide at least one meal a day for her family. The patient who had to forgo his treatment at a hospital because he did not have money in his hands. The student who got his meal at the *langar* in the neighbourhood gurdwara. The farmer who could not buy seeds or fertilisers or hire labour and took a hit on productivity.

Those Utterly Ruined

Who are those who were utterly ruined? The labourer who was laid off in industrial hubs like Tiruppur, Surat and Moradabad. The daily wage earner who could not find work in farms or *mandis* or on construction sites. The self-employed, selling flowers or fruit or *pav-bhaji*, whose customers vanished for several weeks. The artisan plying his trade (carpenter, electrician, plumber) who got no calls. The small businessman whose sales fell by as much as 80 per cent. The truck owner and truck driver whose trucks were idle for several weeks.

Among the worst affected were the farmer-producers whose produce suffered a crash in prices, as will be seen from the table:

Wholesale Market Prices (₹ per quintal) on

	8 November	*14 December*
Tomatoes	2,659	1,920
Potatoes	1,400	924
Peas	3,167	2,864
Cabbages	1,448	964
Cauliflower	1,940	1,079
Carrots	2,247	1,355
Brinjal	1,542	1,086
Spinach	801	526
Guava	2,088	1,802
Oranges	4,081	3,586
Garlic	8,876	8,421
Arhar	6,650	5,935

In the case of tomatoes, carrots and spinach, seasonal factors may have caused a decline in prices. In other cases, it is undeniable that lack of money, and the consequent fall in demand, was a major driver. As far as the farmer-producer is concerned, the loss of income is brutal and final, and no one has come forward to compensate him.

Eleven crore people, on an average, standing in a queue before bank branches and ATMs every day; the promise of being allowed to withdraw up to ₹24,000 every week dishonoured; loss of daily wages or daily income that cannot be recouped; fall in commodity prices for which there will be no compensation; tragic deaths, the number of which is nearing 100—not even a natural calamity could have wreaked such havoc across the country.

Cry, my beloved country, because of an ill-conceived plan that turned into a catastrophe due to incompetent implementation.

CASHLESS ECONOMY—A DISTRACTING MIRAGE

25 December 2016

Every now and then a new word or phrase is introduced into everyday conversation. On 8 November 2016, it was demonetisation. It was portrayed as the white knight on a steed who will slay the demons of black money, corruption and fake currency.

Six weeks later, the demon of *Black Money* continues to flourish. The tax evaders do not seem fazed by demonetisation; they are accumulating black money in the new currency! They have traded their old notes for new notes. According to the Income Tax Department, since demonetisation, it has seized ₹500 crore in cash of which ₹92 crore was in new ₹2,000 notes.

The other demon of *Corruption* is still alive. Officials of the Kandla Port Trust, engineers of the Military Engineering Service, RBI officials, bank and post office officials, and many others have been caught red-handed taking bribes in the new ₹2,000 notes.

The third demon is *Fake Currency*. Just wait for a few months and it will be proved that printing technology is indifferent between the crooks and the RBI. The counterfeiters will soon acquire the technology and challenge the RBI to stay one step ahead.

Panic Attack

The unravelling of demonetisation caused panic in the government. The first sign was when the government and the RBI began to renege on their promises and changed the rules repeatedly (at last count, 62 times!). The value of notes that could be exchanged was raised, then lowered, and it was stopped altogether on 24 November. Indelible ink was used to mark the finger, then discarded. The withdrawal limit of ₹24,000 per week remained only on paper and most people got paltry sums. Permissible use of old notes was abruptly stopped on 15 December. The ultimate panic reaction was when the RBI ordered that one could deposit old notes only once and up to ₹5,000 after 19 December and before 30 December, putting paid to the promises of the Prime Minister and the Finance Minister. The Finance Minister offered lame clarifications. Two days later, the RBI was shamed into reversing its directive.

The Prime Minister realised soon that he had been convinced or conned to buy a lemon. He had no choice but to change the narrative. He propounded the idea of a 'cashless economy'. In his speech on 8 November, the Prime Minister did not once use the word 'cashless'. It was all about 'black money' (18 times) and fake currency (5 times). By 27 November, the Prime Minister shifted gears, and in two speeches that day he mentioned 'cashless' 24 times and 'black money' only 9 times!

'Cashless' economy is not an innocent or harmless goal. It conveys a complete lack of empathy for the poor and those who have minimal or no access to the digital world.

Not a Cashless World

No economy has become 'cashless', not even the most developed economies (see table).

	Cash	Debit Card	Credit Card
			(use in percentage terms)
Australia	65	21	09
Austria	80	15	02
Canada	52	25	20
France	55	30	01
Germany	80	12	02
Netherlands	50	40	01
United States	46	27	19

The value of dollars and euros in circulation has *doubled* since 2005 to $1.48 trillion and €1.1 trillion, respectively. The US and Europe are using more cash, not less cash!

World over, the necessary and desirable rule is that people must have cash in their hands and be able to carry out routine transactions using cash. It is perfectly legitimate for a government to make a law that high-value transactions shall be by cheque or any mode of digital payment—examples are real estate transactions, purchase of high-value jewellery, large contractual payments, debt repayments, payment of certain taxes, etc.

On the other hand, to insist that a farmer shall pay hired labour in digital mode or a homemaker shall buy vegetables by swiping a card is an unwarranted intrusion and puts an oppressive burden upon the payer and the payee. Remember, there is a cost to digital payment that will be borne by the consumer. Subject to a reasonable law concerning high-value transactions, we must have the freedom to choose the mode of payment. That is our right and no government should be allowed to interfere with that right.

A Distracting Mirage

Consumers may be divided into three categories based upon the degree of access to the digital world: real access, minimal access and no access. Seventy-one crore debit cards have been issued so far; in August 2016, these cards were used to withdraw ₹219,657 crore from ATMs, but were used to make payments of only ₹18,370 crore. To put a card or a smartphone in everyone's hand, to provide real access to everyone, and to make everyone adopt the digital mode will require advocacy, education and persuasion, not coercion—and this without restricting the person's fundamental right to use cash.

There is also another important issue—privacy. Why should a young adult be forced to disclose that she bought lingerie or shoes or he bought liquor or tobacco? Why should a couple be forced to leave a trail of a private holiday? Why should an elderly person leave a record that he bought adult diapers or medicines for his ailments? Why should the government or its numerous agencies have access to our lives through access to Big Data? I think these questions need to be debated before the country is pushed into embracing the digital mode for all monetary transactions.

Cashless India is an illusion. It is a distracting mirage. It may not even be a desirable goal.

EPILOGUE

An epilogue appears at the end of a book, but it is possible you may be reading it before you start the book! I would urge you to open the book at any section and read the columns in that section. The 54 columns are a contemporaneous record of the social, economic and political events that shaped the course of the nation in 2016. If you are in the habit of maintaining a diary, this collection can be a companion to your diary.

The end of the year is a good time to reflect on the state of the nation. Was our economy stronger at the end of 2016 than it was at the beginning of the year? Did more people finish school, go to college, find jobs, build homes, start businesses and enjoy healthier lives? Were people happier at the end of the year? These are and must be the concerns of every citizen. When you make your own evaluation, I hope this book will be a useful reference.

ABBREVIATIONS

ABVP	Akhil Bharatiya Vidyarthi Parishad
ADB	Asian Development Bank
AFSPA	Armed Forces (Special Powers) Act
AIADMK	All India Anna Dravida Munnetra Kazhagam
AIUDF	All India United Democratic Front
ASA	Ambedkar Students Association
BCCI	Board of Control for Cricket in India
BIS	Bank for International Settlements
BJD	Biju Janata Dal
BJP	Bharatiya Janata Party
BoPF	Bodoland People's Front
BRICS	BRICS is the acronym for an association of five major emerging national economies: Brazil, Russia, India, China and South Africa.
BSP	Bahujan Samaj Party
CBDT	Central Board of Direct Taxes
CBI	Central Bureau of Investigation
CEA	Chief Economic Adviser
CJI	Chief Justice of India
CLTS	Community-led Total Sanitation
CMIE	Centre for Monitoring Indian Economy
COD	Commercial Operation Date
CPC	Communist Party of China

CPI	Consumer Price Index
CSO	Central Statistics Office
DBT	Direct Benefit Transfer
DGMO	Director General of Military Operations
DMK	Dravida Munnetra Kazhagam
EBR	Extra Budgetary Resource
ED	Enforcement Directorate
EU	European Union
FDI	Foreign Direct Investment
FTII	Film and Television Institute of India
G-20	Group of 20. This is an international forum of governments and central bank governors from 20 major economies.
GFCF	Gross Fixed Capital Formation
GST	Goods and Services Tax
GVA	Gross Value Addition
IAF	Indian Air Force
IB	Intelligence Bureau
ICHR	Indian Council of Historical Research
IEC	Information, Education and Communication
IMF	International Monetary Fund
IPC	Indian Penal Code
IPL	Indian Premier League
ISI	Inter-Services Intelligence
ISIL/ISIS	Islamist State in Iraq and the Levant
J&K	Jammu and Kashmir
JeM	Jaish-e-Muhammed
JIT	Joint Investigation Team
JNU	Jawaharlal Nehru University
LEMOA	Logistics Exchange Memorandum of Agreement
LeT	Lashkar-e-Toiba
LoC	Line of Control

LSA	Logistics Support Agreement
MAC	Multi Agency Centre
MCD	Municipal Corporation of Delhi
MGNREGA	Mahatma Gandhi National Rural Employment Guarantee Act
MoP	Memorandum of Procedure
MP	Member of Parliament
MPC	Monetary Policy Committee
MSP	Minimum Support Price
NASSCOM	National Association of Software and Services Companies
NC	National Conference (The Jammu and Kashmir National Conference is a state political party in the Indian State of J&K.)
NCDRC	National Consumer Disputes Redressal Commission
NCTC	National Counter Terrorism Centre
NDA	National Democratic Alliance
NIA	National Investigation Agency
NIFT	National Institute of Fashion Technology
NITI Aayog	National Institution for Transforming India
NJAC	National Judicial Appointments Commission
NPA	Non-Performing Asset
NSA	National Security Adviser
NSSO	National Sample Survey Organisation
NSG	National Security Guard
OBC	Other Backward Class
PAN	Permanent Account Number
PDP	People's Democratic Party
PHC	Primary Health Centre
PIB	Press Information Bureau
PMG	Project Monitoring Group
PMO	Prime Minister's Office

PoK	Pakistan Occupied Kashmir
PoS	Point of Sale
RAW	Research and Analysis Wing
RBI	Reserve Bank of India
RCA	Rajasthan Cricket Association
RNR	Revenue Neutral Rate
RSS	Rashtriya Swayamsevak Sangh
RTI (Act)	Right to Information Act
SFIO	Serious Frauds Investigation Office
SIMI	Students Islamic Movement of India
SIT	Special Investigation Team
SLP	Special Leave Petition
SNDP	Sree Narayana Dharma Paripalana
SP	Samajwadi Party
TDSAT	Telecom Disputes Settlement Appellate Tribunal
TRAI	Telecom Regulatory Authority of India
UK	United Kingdom
UN	United Nations
US	United States
UIDAI	Unique Identification Authority of India
VAT	Value Added Tax
WPI	Wholesale Price Index
WTO	World Trade Organization
1 core	10 million
1 lakh	100,000